Cambridge Global English

WORKBOOK 10

Ruth Appleton

CAMBRIDGE
UNIVERSITY PRESS

Shaftesbury Road, Cambridge CB2 8EA, United Kingdom

One Liberty Plaza, 20th Floor, New York, NY 10006, USA

477 Williamstown Road, Port Melbourne, VIC 3207, Australia

314–321, 3rd Floor, Plot 3, Splendor Forum, Jasola District Centre, New Delhi – 110025, India

103 Penang Road, #05–06/07, Visioncrest Commercial, Singapore 238467

Cambridge University Press is part of the University of Cambridge.

It furthers the University's mission by disseminating knowledge in the pursuit of education, learning and research at the highest international levels of excellence.

www.cambridge.org
Information on this title: www.cambridge.org/9781009400596

First published 2024

20 19 18 17 16 15 14 13 12 11 10 9 8 7 6 5 4 3 2 1

Printed in Malaysia by Vivar Printing

A catalogue record for this publication is available from the British Library

ISBN 978-1-009-40059-6 Workbook with Digital Access (2 Years)

Additional resources for this publication at www.cambridge.org/go

Contents

How to use this book

This Workbook provides questions for you to practise what you have learned in class. There is a unit to match each unit in your Coursebook.

Tips to help you with your learning.

WRITING TIP

When you are presenting statistics in a report, present only the more important data. To make it easier for the reader to understand the information, present one statistic per sentence.

Information to help you find out more about grammar.

USE OF ENGLISH

Sofia is 15 years old. She lives in Andalucia, Spain. There are 250 students in her school. Her lessons start at 09:00 and finish at 17:00. There is a lunch break from 13:00 to 15:00 when many students go home for lunch. Her school has a two-week holiday in December, two weeks in March or April and around 12 weeks off over the summer. She spends one hour every evening on homework.

Omar is almost 15 years old. He lives in Manchester, England. There are 600 students in his school. His lessons start at 08:30 and finish at 15:30. He has a 45-minute break for lunch. His school usually has a two-week holiday in December, two weeks in the spring and around six weeks off over the summer. He spends one and a half hours every evening on homework.

Check!

1 **Read the information about Sofia and Omar. Circle True or False. Change any false sentences so that they are true.**

Use the Cambridge Learner Corpus to get your grammar right!

GET IT RIGHT!

Remember that in the passive the verb *to be* can be used in all of its forms.

Example:
*A documentary film has **been** made about saving the dolphins.*

There are opportunities to practise your grammar on the Use of English pages in each unit. Each Use of English lesson is divided into three parts:

Focus: These grammar questions help you to master the basics.

Focus

3 **Complete these sentences using the correct comparative forms of the words in the box. Use *a bit, nearly* or *much*. Add the words *as* and *than* if needed.**

early	large	late	long (x2)	short

a Omar's school is .... Sofia's.

b Sofia's lessons start .... Omar's.

c Sofia's summer break is .... Omar's.

d Omar's lunch break isn't .... Sofia's.

e Omar's lessons finish .... Sofia's.

f Sofia's homework time is .... Omar's.

Practice: These grammar questions help you to become more accurate and confident.

Practice

4 **Circle the best option to complete the sentences.**

a **Financial report:** Growth rates were *a bit* / *slightly* higher this quarter than in the previous quarter.

b **Conversation with a friend:** The tickets were *a great deal* / *a lot* more expensive than last time.

c **Academic essay:** One report found that students are *much* / *far* more stressed before exams than at other times.

Challenge: These questions will help you use language fluently and prepare for the next level.

Challenge

5 **Complete the sentences using degrees of comparison. The first one has been done for you.**

a Online learning (very cheap) / learning in a school (very expensive)

Online learning is much cheaper than learning in a school.

b Today's exam (very easy) / yesterday's exam (quite easy)

Today's exam ....

c My brother's English is excellent. His classmates don't speak English well at all.

My brother's English is ....

d This computer is easy to use and so was your old one.

This computer is ....

e This course is extremely difficult. I expected it to be easier.

This course is ....

Questions that help you to think about your learning and progress.

REFLECTION

Write answers to these questions in your notebook.

a Do you think you read enough? How might you benefit from reading more?

b What type of books do you enjoy most? Explain your answer.

c Give an example, other than for studying, when reading has helped you in some way.

d Is there a book that you would like to read but haven't? Why haven't you?

e What do you find hardest about writing a story? How can you improve this?

1 Learning and discovering

Think about it: What are schools like in other countries?

1 **Read four students' opinions of their school. What questions do you think they are all answering?**

a **Lucia**

The teachers at my school are super friendly and supportive. If you miss a class, they always help you catch up. I think it's good that our grades are based on our coursework and class participation throughout the year rather than an exam at the end of each semester. One thing I would change is the length of the half-term holiday. It's only four days, so there's not enough time to get the break we need.

b **Mie**

Our teachers always tell us we have to study hard if we want to graduate and go to a good university to study for a Bachelor's degree or even a Master's degree. They also arrange a lot of talks from different postgraduates. It's very helpful to hear from someone who decided to continue their university studies. We have quite a long school day, but because we spend so much time together at school, we become really good friends. It's where we make friends for life. I think that there are too many students in each class – the teachers don't have time to talk to us individually.

c **Victor**

We have lessons for four hours a day. I go to school in the mornings. In the afternoons, we can choose what activities to do, like drama and music clubs, but there are vocational courses you can do as well, like woodwork or cooking. I think that's really important because going on to higher education and being an undergraduate is not for everyone, is it? My school is really good at showing students that when we finish our compulsory education, further education is a valid option too. One thing I don't like is the school uniform. I think we should wear our own clothes.

d **Mulia**

We start the school day at 7:30 a.m. with a short assembly in the gym for the entire school. After that, students in primary education go off and have lessons from 8:00 a.m. to 1:00 p.m. If you are in secondary education, classes don't finish until 3:00 p.m., with a half-hour break for lunch at 12:00 p.m. If we're late too often we can get a detention during lunch break or after school. Something that could be improved is the school meals.

2 **Complete the sentences with the name of the correct student.**

a .... thinks that talking to others who are studying is helpful.

b .... mentions school for younger students.

c .... mentions two types of university education.

d .... believes a school break is too short.

e .... mentions job training while still at school.

f .... mentions an open attitude about what students can do at the end of secondary education.

g .... is glad not to have big tests before each of the long school holidays.

3 **Find words in the text that match these meanings.**

a Students who study the next level after the Bachelor's degree. ....

b The periods into which a school year is divided. ....

c A higher level university course which can be studied after a Bachelor's degree. ....

d Education below the university level for people who have finished school. ....

e The period when children legally have to attend school. ....

f A student studying the first level of education at university. ....

g All education at university level. ....

4 **Do you agree or disagree with these opinions about school education? If you disagree, change the statement so that you agree with it.**

a Primary education should start at the age of five.

b Secondary education should be compulsory up to the age of 18.

c All students should be required to go into further or higher education.

d The school year should be divided into four semesters lasting two months, with a month's holiday in between each.

e Everyone in secondary education should take a vocational subject as well as academic subjects.

Challenge

5 **Write a short description of your school in your notebook. Use the descriptions in Exercise 1 as a model.**

Psychology and education: What type of learner are you?

1 **Write three tips for revising for your exams.**

....

....

....

2 **Read the article and complete it with words from the box. Then see whether any of your ideas from Exercise 1 are mentioned.**

aural	kinaesthetic	logical	social
solitary	strategies	verbal	visual

Revising for your exams: How to activate your brain

Revising for your exams can be stressful. But there are lots of ways to make it more fun and more effective too. Why not activate your brain by trying some of these creative ways of revising?

Vary your input

In addition to reading your coursework and coursebooks, try using other forms of input. To activate ....[1] input, listen to podcasts about your revision topics. For ....[2] input, make a poster or an online quiz with key words or facts, using different coloured highlighting and illustrations to make them more memorable. Draw concept maps that show the organisation of ideas in a non-linear way. Organising pieces of information in different ways will help you to understand the connections between them.

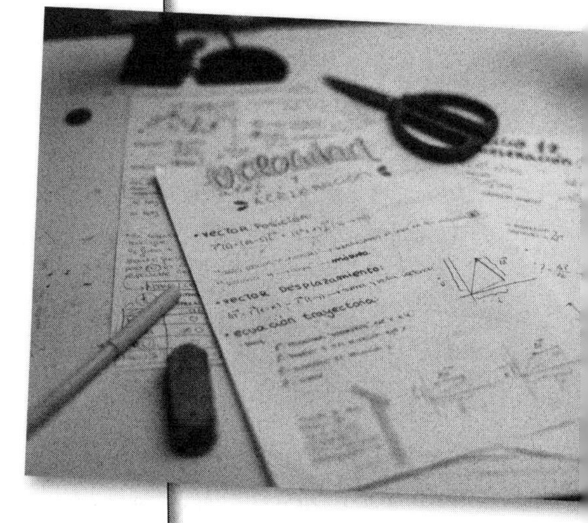

Tell a friend

If you are a ....[3] person, a good way to improve your memory (and make sure you have understood the topic) is to explain the topic to a friend or family member. If you can explain it successfully, it means you have understood it, and also improved your ....[4] communication skills. Even if you tend to be a ....[5] learner, you can try recording yourself explaining to a fictional friend. You might be surprised at how much more confident you will feel!

Get moving

Some students find it easier to store information when they are physically active. Think of ....[6] strategies for interacting with your revision material. This could be writing words on cards and moving them around on the desk or placing them in different places around the room and creating a path that connects them all in a ....[7] way. Of course, taking regular breaks is also very important. Every 20–25 minutes, get up and walk around the room, or drink a glass of water. It'll improve your concentration and your memory.

Reflect on your progress

Try to incorporate space for reflection at the end of every session. When you finish reading a chapter, ask yourself: What did I learn? What strategy helped me most? What did I not really understand that well? What can I do to remember that better? These types of questions will help you develop new ....[8] and make your revision time even more effective.

LANGUAGE TIP

Mnemonics are a useful way to remember key information.
A mnemonic can be an acronym such as HOMES (used to remember the names of the five Great Lakes of North America) or a simple sentence to help with confusing homophones such as (hear – here, see – sea): We h**ear** with our **ear** and we **see** with our **eye**.
What other types of mnemonics do you know?

3 **Underline any strategies in Exercise 2 that you have used. Draw a wavy line under one strategy you might use next time you revise.**

4 **Think about your last revision session. What strategies and skills did you use and how could you vary them next time? Write a paragraph in your notebook.**

Use of English: Degrees of comparison

USE OF ENGLISH

Sofia is 15 years old. She lives in Andalucia, Spain. There are 250 students in her school. Her lessons start at 09:00 and finish at 17:00. There is a lunch break from 13:00 to 15:00 when many students go home for lunch. Her school has a two-week holiday in December, two weeks in March or April and around 12 weeks off over the summer. She spends one hour every evening on homework.

Omar is almost 15 years old. He lives in Manchester, England. There are 600 students in his school. His lessons start at 08:30 and finish at 15:30. He has a 45-minute break for lunch. His school usually has a two-week holiday in December, two weeks in the spring and around six weeks off over the summer. He spends one and a half hours every evening on homework.

Check!

1 **Read the information about Sofia and Omar. Circle True or False. Change any false sentences so that they are true.**

a	Omar is much younger than Sofia.	True	False
b	Sofia's school day is much shorter than Omar's.	True	False
c	Omar's summer break isn't nearly as long as Sofia's.	True	False
d	Sofia's winter break is just as long as Omar's.	True	False
e	Omar's homework takes a bit longer than Sofia's.	True	False

Notice

2 **What do the words *much, (not) nearly, just* and *a bit* add to the meaning? Do they indicate a big difference, a small difference or no difference?**

....

....

....

Focus

3 Complete these sentences using the correct comparative forms of the words in the box. Use *a bit, nearly* or *much*. Add the words *as* and *than* if needed.

early large late long (x2) short

a Omar's school is .... Sofia's.

b Sofia's lessons start .... Omar's.

c Sofia's summer break is .... Omar's.

d Omar's lunch break isn't .... Sofia's.

e Omar's lessons finish .... Sofia's.

f Sofia's homework time is .... Omar's.

Practice

4 Circle the best option to complete the sentences.

a **Financial report:** Growth rates were *a bit / slightly* higher this quarter than in the previous quarter.

b **Conversation with a friend:** The tickets were *a great deal / a lot* more expensive than last time.

c **Academic essay:** One report found that students are *much / far* more stressed before exams than at other times.

Challenge

5 Complete the sentences using degrees of comparison. The first one has been done for you.

a Online learning (very cheap) / learning in a school (very expensive)

Online learning is much cheaper than learning in a school.

b Today's exam (very easy) / yesterday's exam (quite easy)

Today's exam ....

c My brother's English is excellent. His classmates don't speak English well at all.

My brother's English is ....

d This computer is easy to use and so was your old one.

This computer is ....

e This course is extremely difficult. I expected it to be easier.

This course is ....

GET IT RIGHT!

We can use formal or informal language when expressing degrees of similarity or difference.
Use more formal expressions in your essays and written reports.

Informal

a bit, a lot

Semi-formal

a little, much

Formal

slightly, far, a great deal

Use of English: Present simple and present continuous

USE OF ENGLISH

Rasmus, are you going to the gym now? I can't go now. I'm finishing my maths homework.

You know that I usually hand all my homework in late. The teachers are getting angry with me so I'm making a real effort to change.

I want to give this in on time and get a good grade.

You normally run first and then work out, so why don't I meet you there in an hour and we can work out together after your run? I live 5 minutes from the gym, so it's no problem!

Check!

1 **Read the four text messages from Puyan to Rasmus.**
Underline all the verbs written in present simple and present continuous.

Notice

2 **Read the text messages again and answer the questions.**

a What is Puyan doing now? ....

b What is Rasmus doing now? ....

c What bad habit does Puyan have? ....

d What is currently happening between Puyan and his teachers?

....

e What does Puyan want? ....

f What is Rasmus's exercise routine like? ....

3 **Circle the correct word. Use the text and the answers in Exercise 1 to help you.**

a The present *simple / continuous* is used to talk about actions that are in progress.

b The present *simple / continuous* is used to talk about routines and habits.

CONTINUED

c The present *simple / continuous* is used to talk about current situations.

d The present *simple / continuous* is used to talk about permanent situations.

e The present *simple / continuous* is used to talk about desires, feelings and opinions.

Focus

4 Complete the sentences with the correct verb form. Use the verbs from the box.

have	study	think	continue	not agree

a Compulsory education .... until the age of 16.

b I .... of doing my homework in the school library.

c We .... maths lessons five days a week.

d I .... very hard for the test I have tomorrow.

e A lot of students .... that chemistry is slightly easier than physics.

Practice

5 Read the sentences. Write CF (correct, formal), CI (correct, informal) or I (incorrect) for the sentences below. Correct the incorrect sentences.

a I'm looking at your study notes, they ~~are seeming~~ seem very good. [I]

b I'm happy to report that the students love the new swimming pool; they are enjoying learning to swim in a heated pool. [ ]

c The French teacher gave us a book to read – I'm not liking it at all. [ ]

d My sister has gone to Sweden to study. She's absolutely loving it. [ ]

e Due to the fact that students are disliking training in the current bad weather, football practice today will be cancelled. [ ]

GET IT RIGHT!

In very informal situations, people may express their short-lived feelings and emotions in the continuous form. This is not suitable in formal or semi-formal situations or in written English.

Examples:
We are studying medieval history at the moment. It's really interesting – ***I'm loving it****.*

My sister just started university. She's ***hating*** *it at the moment but I'm sure it will get better.*

Challenge

6 Write a paragraph about your studies. Use both the present simple and the present continuous to write about what you are currently studying in different subjects, exams you are preparing for and things you like and dislike, for example.

Improve your writing: A persuasive email

1 **Read the situations. What would you say? Rank the statements A–C in order of preference. Then add one more idea for each situation.**

a You want a friend to help you with your maths homework.

A I can't finish my homework unless you help me. ☐

B If you help me, I'll help you with your English. ☐

C You're so good at maths. I know you'd be an excellent teacher. ☐

D ....

b You would like your brother to come with you to a concert.

A I'm too nervous to go to the concert on my own. ☐

B If you come to the concert, I'll do all your household chores next week. ☐

C This band is so good, you'll definitely have a great time. ☐

D ....

2 **Alina wants to persuade her friend Fatima to come with her to join the chess club. Read her email on the next page. Tick the strategies and types of information (a–j) she includes. Then write the paragraph number(s) where they occur.**

a explains reasons for joining this club ☐ ☐

b suggests providing access to further information ☐ ☐

c mentions shared background information to show empathy ☐ ☐

d explains why she is writing this email ☐ ☐

e uses direct encouragement ☐ ☐

f mentions some spin-off benefits ☐ ☐

g offers a reason for her to refuse, to avoid putting on pressure ☐ ☐

h mentions some drawbacks of joining the club ☐ ☐

i suggests some alternative possibilities ☐ ☐

j uses flattery to strengthen her argument ☐ ☐

From: alina@email.com

To: fatima@email.com

Hi Fatima,

1 How are you and what have you been up to recently? How's your new school? Have you made lots of friends there already? Everything here is the same, except we have a new teacher for maths. She gives us tons of homework and she's really strict!

2 Recently I have been thinking about joining one of the afternoon activity clubs at the youth community centre. Have you ever been there? Do you want to go with me? They have lots of different clubs like drama and dance, but the one I'm really interested in is chess. I've never tried chess before because it looks so difficult, but I read some information about it on the internet and I think it could be really interesting.

3 The club is open to everyone under 16 and you don't need to know how to play. You're so smart, I'm sure you'd pick up all the rules in no time! Of course, I know that you're extremely busy with your schoolwork and preparing for exams, but this would be a chance to take a break and do something completely different. Plus, we could also catch up on all our news! What do you think?

4 I can send you the link to the website if you want. The first meeting is next Thursday. Come on! Please say you'll give it a go!

5 Hoping to hear from you soon, 🙂
Alina

3 **Choose one of these situations and write an email in your notebook. Use some of the strategies in Alina's email.**

a Write an email to a friend persuading them to go with you to a sports club to learn a new sport such as badminton or squash.

b Write a reply to Alina's email explaining why you would rather join a foreign language club and persuading her to go with you.

Check your progress

Vocabulary

1 **Complete the sentences with words from the box.**

compulsory	degree	further
graduate	semester	vocational

a In the UK, it is .... to go to school until the age of 16.

b Most secondary school students have to pass an exam if they want to ....

c Some secondary schools teach .... courses such as mechanics or graphic design.

d In UK universities, the first .... usually runs from September until the end of December.

e Students who don't go to university can take courses at a college of .... education.

f An undergraduate is someone who is studying at university for a Bachelor's ....

2 **Tick the correct words to complete the sentences.**

a Many people believe that the most secure path to a good career is through .... education.

☐ upper ☐ higher ☐ taller

b Students can use their ....-term break either to relax and switch off from their studies or to catch up on their studies if they have fallen behind.

☐ short ☐ long ☐ half

c To be accepted as a .... graduate student, you usually need to have completed an undergraduate qualification.

☐ post ☐ after ☐ higher

Grammar

3 **Correct the mistakes.**

a My new school is not nearly as stricter than my old one.

b Our lessons last year were much more easier than this year.

c My report this term was slightly worse as last term.

d Our summer holiday is a great deal more long than our winter break.

e My school uniform is a lot as nicer than yours.

4 **Circle the correct verb form.**

My studies *take up / are taking*[1] up all my time at the moment, I *am not having / don't have*[2] time for anything else. I *am feeling / feel*[3] tired all the time. I *am thinking / think*[4] of going to the beach for a few days before I start the next semester, so that I can relax a bit. My mum *doesn't want / isn't wanting*[5] to but I *am trying / try*[6] to persuade her.

Reading

5 **Read the paragraph. Summarise the main four points with two to three words for each point.**

Preparing for exams

Revising for exams can be a stressful experience. It can be helpful to look ahead and plan a few strategies for managing your revision time. Perhaps the most important thing to do is to make sure you know what the exam will be like. Firstly, look up past papers and familiarise yourself with the question types and the number of tasks. Study the exam handbook, which will tell you what criteria the examiners will use to evaluate your work. Secondly, it is a good idea to practise past test papers. Time yourself and estimate how much time you will need for each part of the test. Thirdly, identify which areas you are weakest in and set goals for improvement. Studying with a study buddy may help as you can review each other's work. Finally, don't cram all your revision into the last week before the test. Make a revision timetable and space out your work so that you can cover everything in time.

....

....

....

....

6 **Find words in the text in Exercise 5 to match these meanings.**

a become aware of ....

b standards ....

c predict / anticipate ....

d deal with / include ....

Writing

7 **Write an email to a friend. Try to persuade them to come with you to a talk about time management techniques. Write about 150 words in your notebook.**

REFLECTION

Write answers to these questions in your notebook.

a Choose five key words from this unit and write the definitions. Check them with a reliable dictionary.

b Write three sentences comparing your lessons last year and this year. Use degrees of comparison.

c Make a list of six tips for yourself to improve your study routine.

d What new learning strategy do you think you will try after completing this unit?

e How did your writing skills improve in this unit? What did you do well?

2 Into the wild

Think about it: What can we do to help other living creatures?

1 **Look at photos A–D. What are the names of these creatures? Write the name below each photo.**

....

....

....

2 **Read these descriptions and match them with photos A–D.**

....

Endangered species

Endangered animals are species that are at risk of becoming extinct if we don't take steps to protect them. Read about some of these endangered species and how to help them.

a ☐ These are the largest creatures on the planet, weighing as much as 200 tons. They eat tiny marine organisms called krill and play an important role in the marine ecosystem. An adult can eat up to 40 million krill a day. In the past, they were hunted for their oil. As a result, their numbers decreased dramatically from 200,000–300,000 to just 5000–12,000. Today, it is illegal to hunt them, but they are still in danger.

b ☐ These reptiles are one of the oldest species on earth and can live on land or in the sea. They have a bony shell that protects them from ....[1]. They can have an incredibly long ....[2], sometimes as much as 150 years or more. Unfortunately, many of their species are endangered due to loss of habitat, climate change, ocean pollution, accidents with fishing boats and illegal capture for the pet trade.

c ☐ These ....[3] live in a remote region of Africa. They can be 1.2 to 1.5 metres tall and weigh up to 200 kilos. They ....[4] and look for fruit and plants to eat. At night they make ....[5] to sleep in, either in the trees or on the ground. Today there are fewer than 1000 of them, endangered by habitat loss as humans take over their land for farming and by poachers who ....[6] even on protected land and capture them for sale as exotic pets.

d ☐ These are the largest land mammals on earth, and live in Asia and in Africa. Their average lifespan is between 50 and 70 years ....[7], but sadly this is much shorter ....[8] due to the mental stress of being confined in a small area. They are known for their long, curved tusks made of ivory. They use their long trunks to smell food and carry it to their mouths. Males can reach 3 metres tall and weigh 4000–7500 kilograms. This species faces severe threats from illegal poachers and from habitat loss.

3 **Complete 1–8 in the text with words from the box.**

in captivity	in the wild	lifespan	mammals
nests	predators	swing in trees	trespass

4 **Read the texts again and try to guess the meanings of these words. Write synonyms or explanations in your own words.**

a extinct ....

b illegal ....

c capture ....

d remote ....

e poachers ....

Challenge

5 **Research to find the top ten endangered species in the world. Choose one species and write a short description in your notebook using the text in Exercise 2 as a model.**

Science: Can animals talk to each other?

1 **What do you know about bats? Are these statements true or false? Circle the correct answer.**

a	Bats are the only flying mammal.	True	False
b	Their diet consists mainly of insects.	True	False
c	Many fruit plants depend on bats for pollination.	True	False

2 **Skim the article, then answer the question.**

How do bats find their way in the dark?

....

Contrary to popular belief, bats are not blind. In fact, they can see quite well, but because the majority of bats are nocturnal, they have developed other abilities to help them navigate and find food at night.

Bats have highly sensitive hearing and can hear sounds that are **inaudible** to the human ear. Bats use these **ultrasonic** sounds to navigate using a process called echolocation. This is the use of sound and **echoes** to identify the location of objects. Bats emit sounds from their mouth or nose. When the sound wave hits an object, it produces an echo. The echo bounces off the object and returns to the bat's ear, which recognises its own voice. By carefully listening to the echo, the bat can work out not only where the object is but also its size and shape. This ability is so sophisticated that bats can even find a mosquito – one of their favourite snacks – in the middle of a pitch-black cave.

Bats use different types of sounds for different purposes. They have different calls for searching and feeding. They also use sounds to communicate with each other. They are social animals and like to gather in large colonies. And they are very **chatty**! It's possible to record their sounds and process them electronically. It turns out that their communication system is very sophisticated. They use a variety of sounds to convey different messages to each other. Each bat species has its own unique call pattern and individuals can recognise each other's call. A mother bat can easily identify the call of her young from among thousands of bats. Baby bats learn to **mimic** their mother's call, something that very few other animal species can do.

There is still a lot that we can learn about bats. Not only have researchers found that echolocation can help the visually impaired, but they also hope that understanding the subtle complexities of bat communication may lead to a better understanding of how other animals communicate.

inaudible: cannot be heard

ultrasonic: sound waves at a frequency above human hearing

echo: a sound that is heard after it is reflected off another object

chatty: liking to communicate a lot in a friendly, informal way

mimic: copy

3 **Read the text. Then answer these questions.**

a Why do bats need echolocation?

....

b What does echolocation tell them about their surroundings?

....

c Why do researchers have to analyse bat sounds electronically?

....

d What is special about bats' system of communication?

....

e What is one way that bats have helped people?

....

4 **Draw a diagram in your notebook to illustrate the process of echolocation.**

Challenge

5 **Choose a species from one of the groups in the list below and find out how they communicate. What do they communicate about? Write a paragraph in your notebook to explain it.**

- marine animals
- amphibians
- reptiles
- birds

Use of English: Comparing and contrasting ideas

USE OF ENGLISH

Iguanas and chameleons

Both iguanas and chameleons are types of lizard. Like iguanas, chameleons can be found in a variety of habitats including tropical rainforests, swamps and deserts. However, there are many differences between them. Iguanas live in Central and South America, whereas chameleons live in Africa and some parts of South Asia. Iguanas have green skin, while chameleons are able to change their skin colour to red, pink or blue. Chameleons have a fairly short life span of 4–8 years, while iguanas can live up to 20 years or more in the wild. Iguanas are herbivores and mainly eat leaves and plants. Chameleons, however, are carnivores. They mainly eat insects, but larger chameleons can also eat birds and other lizards. Chameleons are an endangered species due to habitat destruction. Similarly, iguanas are also under threat.

Check!

1 **Read the information about iguanas and chameleons. Underline the words that express comparisons and contrasts.**

Notice

2 **Use the words you have underlined in the text above to answer these questions.**

a Which words express comparison? ....

b Which words express contrast? ....

c What are two different ways of positioning the word 'however' in a sentence?

....

Focus

3 **Circle the correct word to complete each sentence.**

a Amphibians are creatures that can live both on water and on land. *Like* / *Whereas* mammals, they can breathe oxygen.

b Leopards cannot run as fast as cheetahs. *Similarly* / *However*, they are good climbers and can swim well too.

c Tortoises are adapted for life on land, *whereas / however* turtles spend most of their time in water.

d *Unlike / Like* the flamingo, the ostrich is a bird that cannot fly. It can run, *however / although*, at speeds of over 40 miles per hour.

Practice

4 Correct the mistakes in these sentences. One sentence is correct.

a Both leopards and cheetahs are fast runners. Although cheetahs are taller.

b Snakes have a life span of 2–8 years, however frogs have a life span of up to 30 years.

c Penguins are not able to fly. Instead, they are excellent swimmers.

d Although most mammals give birth to live young, the platypus lays eggs.

Challenge

5 Write sentences to compare and contrast alligators and crocodiles. Use the words in the box and information in the chart. Write the sentences in your notebook.

although	but	however	like	similarly	unlike	whereas	while

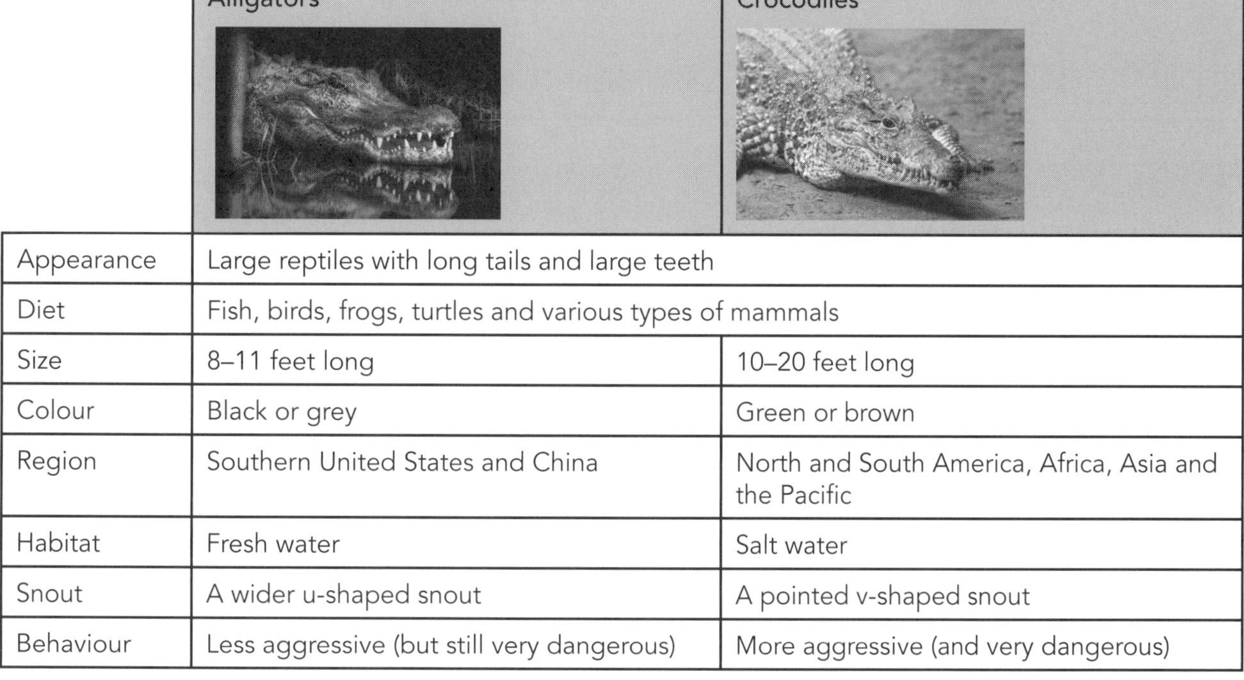

	Alligators	Crocodiles
Appearance	Large reptiles with long tails and large teeth	
Diet	Fish, birds, frogs, turtles and various types of mammals	
Size	8–11 feet long	10–20 feet long
Colour	Black or grey	Green or brown
Region	Southern United States and China	North and South America, Africa, Asia and the Pacific
Habitat	Fresh water	Salt water
Snout	A wider u-shaped snout	A pointed v-shaped snout
Behaviour	Less aggressive (but still very dangerous)	More aggressive (and very dangerous)

GET IT RIGHT!

While and *whereas* connect two clauses within the same sentence.

Example:
Chimpanzees use violence to defend their territory, ***whereas*** *gorillas are more tolerant.*

However and *similarly* contrast and compare information in the sentence they are in with information in a previous sentence.

Example:
Gorillas tolerate other gorillas entering their territory. ***However,*** *they will defend the centre of their land if threatened.*

Use of English: The passive

USE OF ENGLISH

Help to save the sea turtles!

Nearly all species of sea turtle are now classified as endangered. In the past, they were hunted for their eggs, meat and shells. Today, hunting turtles has been banned, but their habitat is being destroyed by overdevelopment, overfishing, pollution and by climate change. Turtles are a vital part of the ocean's ecosystem. They need to be protected. Join us in our fight to save the sea turtles from extinction. With your help, their population will be restored.

Check!

1 **Read the information about sea turtles. Underline verbs that are in the passive form.**

Notice

2 **How many different tenses in the passive form can you find? How are they different?**

....

....

Focus

3 **Circle the correct words to complete the sentences.**

a The number of elephants *has declined* / *been declined* dramatically over the last 100 years.

b More areas of land *are going to be protected* / *are going to protect* to save species from extinction.

c Many pandas that were raised in captivity *are been* / *are being* reintroduced into the wild.

d The sea temperatures *have risen* / *have been risen*, which endangers many species of fish.

e For the first time, koalas *will be listed* / *will list* as an endangered species in Australia.

Practice

4 Correct the mistakes in these sentences.

a In the past, crocodiles was killed for their skin.

b We rescued a baby wolf that had been bit.

c Pandas are been kept in protected areas.

d Several baby elephants have been took to our elephant sanctuary.

e We are working to ensure that these species will being saved from extinction.

5 Complete the text using the correct passive or active form of verbs from the box.

decline	form	hunt	introduce	kill	maintain	protect	rise

The North American bison

In the 1800s, tens of millions of bison, also known as buffalo, lived on the great plains of North America. They ....[1] for their meat and skin by Native Americans, in ways that ensured their numbers ....[2]. But in the 1700s, two new things ....[3] by Europeans: the horse and the rifle. This combination, together with the growing demand for buffalo skin, meant that buffalo ....[4] in massive numbers. They ....[5] from 30 million to just over 1000 in 1890. In 1905, the American Bison Society ....[6] by the US president and others who were worried that bison would disappear. Since then, both public and private organisations have been working to ensure that bison ....[7]. Today, the wild bison population of North America ....[8] to around 420,000, with around 20,000 of them living in the wild.

GET IT RIGHT!

Remember that in the passive the verb *to be* can be used in all of its forms.

Example:
A documentary film has ***been*** *made about saving the dolphins.*

Remember that in irregular verbs the past participle is not always the same as the past tense form.

Example:
The film-makers were ***given*** *access to data from nature reserves.* (not *gave*)

Challenge

6 Find out about a species that was at risk of becoming extinct but has been successfully protected and is no longer considered to be at risk. Write a short description in your notebook of how it was protected, using passives where appropriate.

Improve your writing: A TV documentary review

1 **Read the following first lines from three reviews. Which one would you most like to read and why?**

A The life cycle of a wasp may not at first seem to be the most exciting of subjects for a documentary.

B I watched this documentary because I am worried about so many wildlife species being endangered.

C Filmed in the stunning rainforests of Rwanda, this fascinating documentary examines the life of a mountain gorilla.

2 **Read the film review. Then answer the questions.**

Review of the week

1 *The Secret Life of Foxes* tells the story of three fox cubs as they grow up on a nature reserve in Canada. Filmed over the course of one year and told through the eyes of one of the foxes, we see them first when they are just a few weeks old and end by seeing them as fully grown adults starting to raise a family of their own. Instead of just focusing on the foxes' behaviour, it shows the delicate ecosystem that exists between these animals and their environment.

2 In this unique film, all the animals are wild and the film-makers have not used any tricks or digital special effects to enhance the images. They certainly must have had incredible patience as well as excellent technical skills to get such perfect close-up shots of the foxes in their natural habitat, even inside their underground dens. I personally loved the scenes of fox cubs playing and chasing each other in the snow. Some viewers might find it artificial to have the story told from the perspective of one of the foxes, but I found that it gave me a better understanding of their world.

3 In comparison with other nature documentaries, this film tends to have a fairly slow pace. However, much of the information is conveyed through strong visuals, while the narration adds an interesting layer of humour and charm to the story. I recommend this film to any nature or wildlife enthusiast, and for viewers who are thinking of creating their own wildlife documentary in the future, this is a film not to be missed.

Write the correct paragraph number. In which paragraph does the writer…

a compare the film with other similar programmes? ☐

b explain why the film is unique? ☐

c explain why the writer watched it? ☐

d express a personal opinion? ☐

e give a summary of the main story? ☐

f give details of specific scenes? ☐

g mention something viewers might not like? ☐

h say who would enjoy this film? ☐

3 **Complete this table in your notebook with notes from the review.**

Summary of main topic	
Unique aspects of the film	
Things some viewers might not like	

4 **Choose a documentary that you have seen and make notes for a review. Use the diagram below.**

Title of film: ....

Topic	....
Summary of story	....
Unique aspects of the film	....
Some things viewers might not like	....
Something you liked or disliked in the film	....
My opinion	....
Who would enjoy this film	....

5 **Use your notes to write a review in your notebook.**

Check your progress

Vocabulary

1 **Complete the text with words from the box.**

captivity	captured	extinct	illegal
life span	mammals	nature reserves	
poachers	predators	trespass	

Lions in Africa

The lion is one of the strongest and most dangerous ....[1] on earth. A century ago, there were more than 200,000 lions roaming the plains of Africa. Now there are fewer than 23,000 and they are in danger of becoming ....[2].

Lions have no ....[3] other than humans, but they face threats from habitat loss and from hunters. Although hunting lions is ....[4] in some African countries, there are also some countries that allow it. And despite the establishment of ....[5] where lions are protected, there are still ....[6] who ....[7] on their land in order to hunt and kill the lions. Some lions have been ....[8] to live in zoos around the world. The average ....[9] of a lion is about 16 years in the wild. In ....[10], they can live longer, up to 25 years.

Grammar

2 **Circle the correct compare and contrast words. Complete the gaps with the passive form of the verbs provided.**

Bees and wasps

People sometimes confuse honeybees and wasps because both of them are yellow and black in colour. *Like / While* bees[1], wasps are oval in shape and about 2 cm in size. *However / While*[2] bees ....[3] (usually, see) from spring until late summer, wasps are more common in late summer. *Unlike / Whereas*[4] wasps, bees are furry, *while / however*[5] wasps have little or no hair. Bees feed on nectar from flowers, *in contrast / whereas*[6] wasps eat small insects. Bees are very important in our ecosystem and without them many plants and fruits ....[7] (pollinate). *In comparison / Similarly*[8] to bees, wasps are more aggressive and can sting you several times. Once you ....[9] (sting) by a bee, however, you need not fear any more stings, as the bee will die. Most bees and wasps are not endangered species, but in recent years, their numbers ....[10] (seriously, reduce) due to the use of pesticides on farms.

Reading

3 **Read the email. Then answer the questions.**

From: rob@email.com

To: leo@email.com

Hi Leo,

How are you and how was your summer break? I had the most fantastic time on my trip to Thailand. We volunteered for a week at a turtle conservation centre on the coast. Turtle numbers are seriously declining due to pollution, climate change and too many tourists. On the first day, we went on a beach patrol with a trained biologist, who explained how turtles nest and lay their eggs on the beach. We learnt how to identify their nests and make sure they are safe. Sometimes we had to relocate them away from human activity. We also took care of injured turtles back at the centre. When they are better, they are taken back to the ocean and released into the wild again. We also learnt to tag turtles so that their movements can be tracked. Turtles are such fascinating creatures and there is so much to learn about them. I really want to go back there again! I've got loads of pictures. Let's meet up soon and I can tell you more about it!

Take care,

Rob

a What is the purpose of Rob's email?

....

b Why does Rob mention climate change?

....

c What is implied about threats to turtles' eggs?

....

d What would you find most interesting about this kind of volunteer activity?

....

Writing

4 **Write an email to a friend in your notebook. Try to persuade them to come with you to volunteer for a day at a wildlife refuge or nature reserve. Include details about:**

- the place
- the purpose
- the types of task you will do.

REFLECTION

Write answers to these questions in your notebook.

a How has this unit made you think differently about wild animals?

b Choose two different places in the country where you live. Write a short paragraph comparing them. Use phrases for contrast and comparison from this unit.

c How has your town or city changed over the last five years? Write three sentences using passive forms.

d What can you do to help endangered species? List three ideas.

e What did you learn about writing a review of a nature documentary? What did you do well? What could you improve?

3 Everyday science

Think about it: We need more young scientists!

1 **Complete the information in the school flyer using the words and phrases from the box. Do any of the subjects sound interesting to you?**

analyse	carry out	CO_2 levels	collecting data	compare and contrast
infectious disease	make predictions	mix chemical solutions	prove	

Science department open day

Choosing to study the science programme in high school may be a lot more interesting and diverse than you expect.

In chemistry, of course, you will have to learn the periodic table and understand what happens when you ....[1] together, but your chemistry lessons will come to life with a field trip to a water treatment facility and a forensic science workshop to show how chemistry is used to solve crimes. In the workshop, the class will be given a case study to investigate. Different groups will ....[2] chemical experiments in order to ....[3] samples taken from a pretend crime scene and try to solve the crime. Each group will try to ....[4] and defend their own theory about how the crime happened while disproving the other groups' theories.

Biology classes will not be limited to learning from a textbook either. You will have the opportunity to study some microbiology, for example, by playing a video game in which you have to stop the spread of an ....[5]. By ....[6] about how quickly the bacteria reproduces and how easily it spreads in different groups of people, you will ....[7] about the most successful method for controlling the disease.

In physics, you will also apply theory to real-life problems. You will ....[8] information about ....[9] around the planet and apply your understanding of how energy and heat are transferred to gain a deeper understanding of climate change and global warming.

So join us next year on the science programme for an exciting scientific adventure! If you want more information or have specific questions, you can come along to our open day on 21 May between 16:00 and 18:00 in the science department.

2 **Read the text again. Then answer the questions.**

In which class will you…

a look at data about a gas in the atmosphere? ....

b study very small living organisms that you cannot see? ....

c try to show that someone has the wrong answer? ....

d look for differences and similarities in data? ....

e leave the classroom so you can learn something? ....

Challenge

3 **Write a paragraph about a science class, workshop or field trip that you enjoyed and what you learnt from it.**

....

....

....

....

....

....

Science: We can't live without science

1 **What basic hygiene routines do photos A–E show? When is it important to follow each of these routines?**

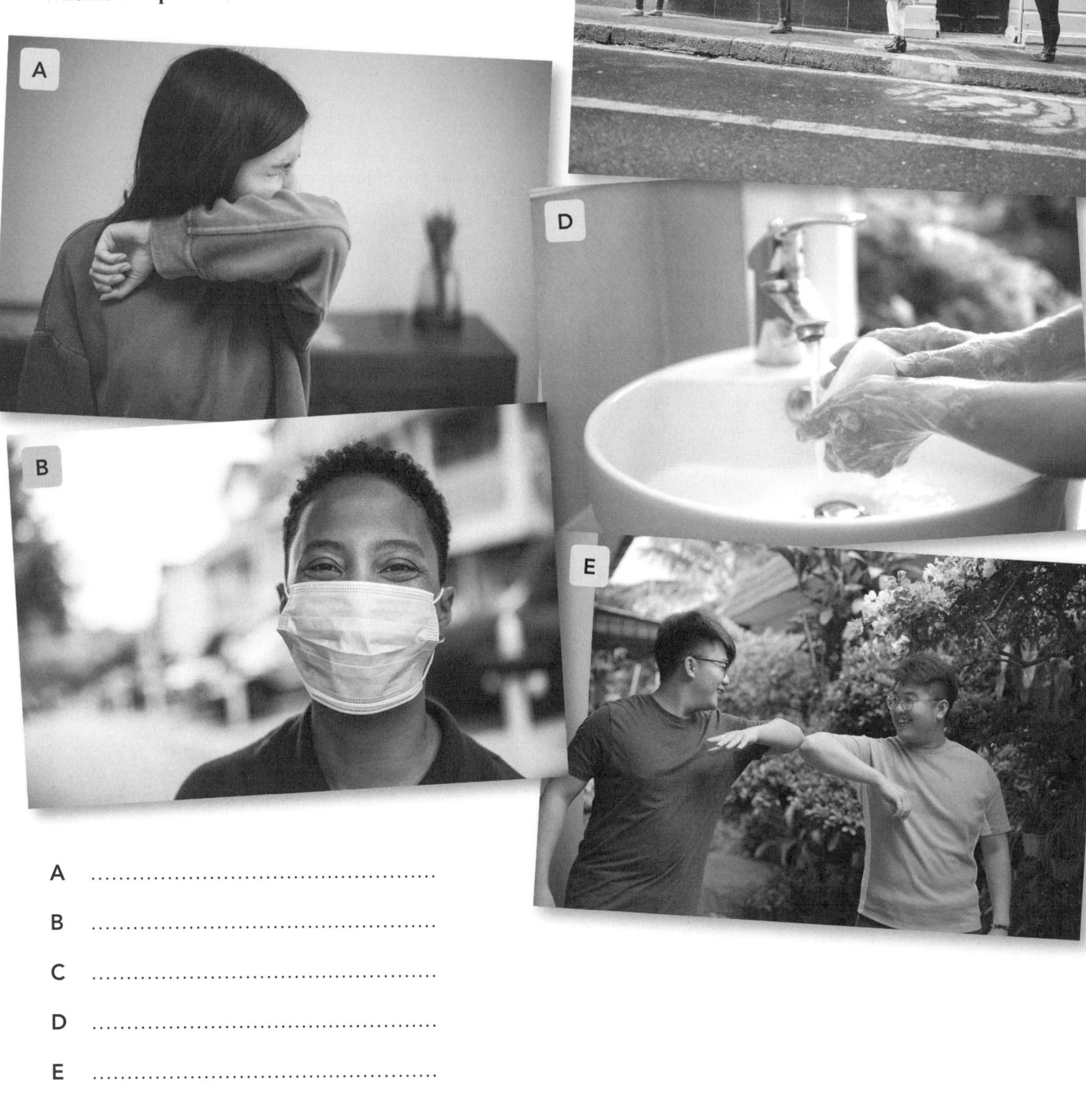

A ....

B ....

C ....

D ....

E ....

....

....

2 **Read the article. Then check your answer in Exercise 1 about when it is important to wash our hands.**

The science of soap

Most of us are familiar with the fact that washing our hands well with soap and water can help to prevent the spread of diseases. We have all observed how soap removes dirt from our hands, but have you ever really analysed how soap helps to remove bacteria, viruses, or other microorganisms that cause infectious diseases from our skin? Microbiologist Edwa Okoro looks at the chemistry of soap to explain its role in getting things clean.

'Soap is made up of **molecules** that are attracted to water at one end and attracted to fats and oils at the other end,' explains Okoro. When soap is rubbed into hands, the soap is attracted to the oils and fats found in the surfaces of many viruses and bacteria, which causes the soap to surround the microorganisms and lift them off the skin. At the same time, the soap molecules are attracted to water; therefore, the soap, together with the viruses and bacteria trapped within it, attaches to the water and is washed away, removing the microorganisms from the skin.

Of course, water will remove some microorganisms on its own, simply by force, but soap and water are much more effective and the soap will also help to ensure that the microorganisms wash down the drain rather than being transferred to other surfaces. In some cases, the soap will also actually kill the virus or bacteria by destroying the microorganism's surface.

So there are various reasons why it is always best to wash your hands with soap and water if you can, but Okoro emphasises that washing your hands just with water when soap is not available is much better than not washing them at all. She recommends always washing your hands before meals, before taking medicines or cleaning or covering wounds and after using the bathroom. Furthermore, she adds that soap works in the same way on dishes and clothes so should be used in all types of washing.

3 **Read the article again. Then answer these questions.**

a Why is the fact that soap attracts fats and oils important in preventing disease?

....

b How can washing only with water help in the absence of soap?

....

c As well as removing microorganisms from the skin, how else can soap help to protect us from microorganisms?

....

molecule: the simplest unit of a chemical substance, made of atoms

Challenge

4 **Look up the definition of chemistry and explain why Edwa Okoro used chemistry to explain how soap works. Think of two more daily activities that can be explained through chemistry.**

....

....

....

Use of English: Zero and first conditionals

USE OF ENGLISH

Hi Max,

Thanks for agreeing to babysit Reza on Friday.

I just want to remind you about his allergies. If he drinks too much milk, he gets strong stomach pains. It takes a couple of hours to go away if he has a strong reaction. If he eats raw egg, he may develop small red spots on his skin. You can call us anytime if there is something you are unsure about.

Thanks for suggesting to take him for an ice cream. Because of his allergies, would it be possible to take him for a picnic instead? If you think it's a good idea, I will get plenty of snacks that he can eat. That way you won't have to worry. How about meeting in the park next to the pizzeria at 5 o'clock?

Let me know what you think.

Nora

Check!

1 **Read the email above. Underline the examples of zero and first conditionals. Which examples refer to situations that are always true and which to a possible situation in the future?**

Always true: ....

....

Possible future situations: ....

....

Notice

2 **Read the text again. Match the verb patterns (a–b) with the type of conditional sentences (i–ii).**

a	present tense + present tense	i	first conditional
b	present tense + will (or modal) verb	ii	zero conditional

3 **Find the conditional sentences in the text that have a comma in them, then tick the correct rule.**

A Use a comma when the sentence starts with the *if* part of the conditional. ☐

B Use a comma when the sentence ends with the *if* part of the conditional. ☐

Focus

4 Match the beginning of sentences a–e with the correct ending (i–v).

a If you go for an allergy test,

b You should always ask about food allergies

c If you think you are allergic to something,

d You may need to always carry medicine with you

e If a person has a food allergy,

i if someone eats at your house for the first time.

ii the doctor will ask what foods you ate in the week prior to your reaction.

iii if you have a strong allergy.

iv he or she can still enjoy a varied and balanced diet.

v you should see a doctor.

Practice

5 Find and correct the mistakes. Two sentences are correct.

a If you will develop an allergy, doctors will carry out tests to find out what you are allergic to.

b You have a slightly higher chance of developing a food allergy if you or someone in the family suffer from asthma.

c I will call the emergency services if one of the students has a strong allergic reaction during the field trip.

d If someone in the meeting tomorrow says they have a food allergy, I check what options the restaurant can offer before I book.

GET IT RIGHT!

Remember that the verb *will* only appears in the main clause of a sentence in the first conditional and never appears in the *if* clause. *Will* is not used in the zero conditional.

Examples:

If you have a food allergy, you ~~will~~ have to be very careful about what you eat.

If you ~~will~~ come to visit, I ***will*** *take you to a vegan restaurant so we don't have to worry about your milk allergy.*

Challenge

6 Choose a food you are not currently allergic to but that you and your family eat a lot of. Write a paragraph in your notebook about what will change for you and your family if you develop an allergy in the future. Think about family holidays and celebrations, as well as your daily meals.

Use of English: Reporting survey results – expressing statistics

USE OF ENGLISH

The results of the survey show that the vast majority of students in Year 11 are planning on studying some form of science next year. Fifty percent will study one science subject next year, a third will study two science subjects, while hardly anyone will study all three science subjects. The main reason for this seems to be a timetable problem. Two in 10 students said they will study all three science subjects if the timetable problem is resolved. Furthermore, slightly over 25% find studying sciences challenging and said they will attend extra classes if the school continues to provide them next year.

Check!

1 **Read the text. Underline six results from the survey.**

Notice

2 **Which three results are expressed using approximate numbers?**

....

3 **Which three results are expressed using exact numbers?**

....

Focus

4 **Circle the correct words in the second sentence to best express the statistic given in the first sentence.**

a Twenty-two students from a class of forty-four chose to study biology.

Fifty percent / *about half* of the students chose to study biology.

b The Earth's surface is 29% land and 71% water.

Almost three quarters / *exactly three quarters* of the Earth's surface is covered in water.

c Ten of the 30 seeds we planted grew.

Very few / *A third* of the seeds we planted grew.

d Nitrogen makes up 78% of the Earth's atmosphere.

Nitrogen makes up *the majority* / *three-quarters* of the Earth's atmosphere.

Practice

5 Correct the mistake in each sentence.

a One of 4 students say they would like a job in science later in life.

b Nine out off 10 students passed their exams.

c Half out of the teachers recommend continuing with science studies.

d Hardly none of the students wish to drop all the science subjects.

e For those who plan on studying physics, near all will also study advanced maths.

Challenge

6 Look at the statistics in the table. Write four sentences about the key features using either approximate numbers or exact number expressions. Sixty students were interviewed.

	Yes	No	Unsure
Do you enjoy studying science?	40	15	5
Do you think science is important in your daily life?	47	11	2
Do either of your parents have a science-related job?	27	30	3

a ....

b ....

c ....

d ....

GET IT RIGHT!

When learning different ways of expressing numbers, learn the whole phrase and pay particular attention to which prepositions are used.

Examples:
Hardly any of *my friends study science.*

Half ***of*** *the class wanted to go on a science field trip and the other half wanted to go to an art museum.*

One ***in*** *four of the class presentations were about microbiology.*

Improve your writing: Report – survey results

1 **Read the writing task.**
Then write down two more ideas for why participation may have been low.

> Your school recently offered a science field trip but very few students participated. Your science teachers would like to know why. You have been asked to interview students and write a report based on your findings. Your report should include recommendations for how to increase participation in the future.
>
> Here are two comments from students:
>
> - I never heard about a science field trip, but it sounds really interesting.
> - I couldn't go because I had exams that week. I was really disappointed.
>
> The comments above may give you some ideas, and you can also use some ideas of your own.
>
> Your report should be between 150 and 200 words long.

....

....

2 **Complete the model report on the next page using the phrases from the box.**
Were either of your ideas from Exercise 1 mentioned in the model?

I suggest taking the following steps	A small but significant minority	I recommend offering	in the final paragraph	My findings are presented below

3 **Read the model report again. Which point on the checklist has not been followed?**
Write the sentence or phrase you would include to correct it.

- ✓ Use headings for each section.
- ✓ State the aim of the report in the introduction.
- ✓ Use formal language.
- ✓ Provide findings of your survey or research.
- ✓ Finish with recommendations for future action based on findings.
- ✓ Use bullet points or lists to present findings and recommendations.

WRITING TIP

When you are presenting statistics in a report, present only the more important data. To make it easier for the reader to understand the information, present one statistic per sentence.

4 **Read the writing task and your ideas in Exercise 1 again. Write your own answer in your notebook. Use similar phrases to those listed in Exercise 2. Use the checklist in Exercise 3 to structure your report.**

Student participation in science field trips

Introduction

I interviewed students about the recent science field trip. ....[1] and relevant recommendations are given ....[2].

Low participation

A science field trip was offered to Years 9–11. I interviewed ten students from each year group. The vast majority said the field trip sounded interesting and they felt they would have benefited from it. Ninety percent of Year 11 students said they were unable to attend because it coincided with their exam week. Slightly over a quarter felt the trip was too expensive. ....[3] said they received no information about the trip. Nearly all the students claimed they will attend if the same trip is offered again and the issues mentioned here are addressed.

Recommendations

Taking all the points into consideration, ...[4] in the future:

- check possible trip dates against important exam periods
- reduce the price
- announce the information on several occasions and publish it on the science department's webpage.

On a final note, it is important not to interpret the low participation as a lack of interest. ....[5] this trip again as student interest is high.

Check your progress

Vocabulary

1 **Complete the sentences with phrases from the box.**

collect data	compared and contrasted	disprove my theory	CO_2 levels	stem cells	make predictions

a Rising .... in the atmosphere are a major cause of climate change.

b Doctors are increasingly focusing on .... to see whether they can help people heal from injuries.

c Scientific experiment results must be .... in order to reach meaningful conclusions.

d Many have tried to .... but have not succeeded because the facts are all there!

e Scientists .... based on facts and data rather than ideas and rumours.

f My job is to .... and theirs is to interpret the numbers.

Grammar

2 **Write the letter of the end (i–iv) next to the correct beginning (a–d) to complete the conditional sentences.**

a If the chemicals are mixed in the right order, ☐

b If you study science in high school, ☐

c If the proper safety measures are not taken into account, ☐

d If the students do not complete the science project on time, ☐

i laboratories can be dangerous.

ii later on you may be able to specialise and work in zoology or ecology.

iii the experiment will be a success.

iv they receive a lower grade.

3 **Complete the sentences with phrases from the box.**

nearly all	slightly more than	very few

a .... children aged 8–12 years old are curious about science.

b The students completed the science project in .... four hours.

c .... scientific discoveries become general knowledge in the wider community.

Reading

4 **Read the information.**
Then read the statements and circle True or False.

Meteorologists do more than present the weather on TV. If you are interested in the weather and climate but hate standing in front of a camera, you can still be a meteorologist. The vast majority of people in this field do not work in the media at all.

A high percentage provide weather-related advice to other professionals for whom the weather is important. Early warnings about approaching thunderstorms, heavy snowfalls and strong winds are essential to airlines, road maintenance crews and emergency services, for example. Meteorologists also help city planners and architects by analysing data and predicting how climate may affect buildings in certain areas.

An increasing number of weather professionals work in research, studying climate change and extreme weather patterns. They compare and contrast data collected over many decades and provide important predictions about what may happen in the future.

Some meteorologists, although not many, even work with detectives. Forensic meteorologists help in investigations where weather may have caused or influenced traffic accidents or fires, for example.

So as you can see, meteorologists have endless employment opportunities, far beyond the daily weather forecast.

a Most weather-related jobs focus on providing daily weather forecasts for the general public. True False

b Various industries benefit from the information meteorologists provide about extreme weather conditions. True False

c Meteorologists are not involved in efforts to gain a better understanding of global warming and related problems. True False

d Meteorologists all work on short term predictions, hardly ever thinking about more than the next week's weather. True False

e Weather experts may be asked to help prove or disprove theories about how extreme weather conditions can provoke dangerous incidents. True False

Writing

5 **Based on your own experience, write a report in your notebook about what students find challenging when studying science and what could help to overcome these challenges.**

REFLECTION

Write answers to these questions in your notebook.

a Are science subjects popular at your school? Why or why not?

b List two occasions not mentioned in the text in the 'We can't live without science' lesson when it is important to wash your hands with soap.

c Make a list of the food people are often allergic to.

d When do you look at the weather forecast and why?

e What features can be used to make reports easier for the reader to understand?

4 The world of art

Think about it: Exploring different types of art

1 **Complete the texts using words from the box.**

abstract art · conductors · dance moves · form a band · in the spotlight · live audience · paints, colours and brushes · physically demanding · publish a novel · redraft · rhythms · sketch

Musicians are not usually seen as people who worry much about their health or keeping in shape. However, the physical effort involved in playing music is often overlooked by non-musicians. Long recording sessions, rehearsals and concerts are not only challenging for the mind, but are also very ....[1]. Take drummers, for example, playing complex ....[2] or guitarists maintaining unnatural hand positions throughout an entire song. If you do stop and reflect on these things, you can soon understand why many special stretching and muscle-building exercises must be taught at music schools so that instrumentalists don't suffer serious injuries. Singers who perform in front of a ....[3] also need to be in top form. Singing while performing ....[4], and with the added pressure of being ....[5], is exhausting. Even orchestra ....[6] get tired from waving their batons! So, if you have plans to ....[7], maybe you should consider taking a ball to kick around in rehearsal breaks or getting on a bike to go to the studio!

Every artist goes through a creative process when they work, to turn an idea into a work of art. No two creative processes are the same and one is never better than another. For example, more conventional painters will usually have a very long process in which they ....[8] the outline for the painting and carefully consider which ....[9] to use. Meanwhile, painters that make ....[10] might only need an idea and an inspiring environment to get to work. The same applies to writers: some need to draft and ....[11] their work many times before they actually ....[12]; others have editors to check their work; while some writers don't even have their work spell-checked!

2 Underline the words in the texts that refer to people's professions. Look at how the words end and complete the table. Can you think of another profession for each suffix?

-or	-er	-ist	-cian

3 Read the texts again. Which title best reflects the theme that connects them?

A The difficulties of being an artist ☐

B The unknown sides of the world of art ☐

C The undervalued world of art ☐

Challenge

4 Choose an artistic profession from the table. Write a paragraph in your notebook about the way in which their work is physically demanding or about the creative process their work may involve.

Art and design: Architecture – an important art form

1 **Do you consider architecture an art form? Why or why not? Read paragraph A. Why does the writer consider architecture an art form?**

....

A If you were asked to list all the different art forms, architecture may not be one of the first things to spring to mind. However, the essence of all art is to move beyond what is functional and use imagination and skill to create something that causes an emotional reaction in the viewer. Great architecture does this. Who would dare to stand in front of the Alhambra in Granada, Spain or the Taj Mahal in Agra, India and say they are not works of art?

B Although buildings are designed primarily to shelter the people and things inside them, most architects, when given the freedom and resources to do so, aim to create buildings that will cause an emotional reaction in those that see and use them. They look beyond the functional role of the building and hope to communicate through the bricks, concrete and glass, in the same way that painters aim to communicate through the colours and features of a painting. Throughout history, architects have aimed to create a feeling of **balance** and **harmony**, both as an expression of beauty but also to improve the wellbeing of those who use the building, in a similar way to musicians when they compose music.

C In response to the environmental challenges we currently face, architects have new problems to overcome that require truly creative solutions. Now more than ever, we need buildings to communicate a feeling of **togetherness** and connection both between people and with nature. We need buildings that have a positive effect on the wellbeing of the individuals and communities that use them. We need buildings that are in harmony with the planet that we live on. We need buildings that are constructed with skill, passion and deep understanding of their psychological impact. How will architects achieve this? They will need to use a combination of technical and artistic skills and a strong desire to communicate something meaningful through the objects they create.

2 **Which of the words in bold refers to ...**

a a pleasant feeling of being united in friendship and or understanding? ....

b a state when things are equal? ....

c a state when things are well matched and work together easily? ....

3 **Read the whole text. Then answer the questions.**

a Based on the information in paragraph A, what do you think is the purpose of the article?

....

b Why does the writer compare architects to painters and musicians in paragraph B?

....

c In paragraph C, the writer says that in response to environmental challenges architects face new problems. What challenges do you think they might be?

....

d In paragraph C, why did they repeat the start of three sentences with 'We need buildings that…'?

....

Challenge

4 **Choose a building that you like. In your notebook, write a short text to persuade the reader why it should be considered a work of art.**

Use of English: Modal verbs and other phrases of probability

USE OF ENGLISH

The arts, in its broadest sense, is not limited only to the creation of artwork but also includes creative writing, dance, theatre and music. It is one of the most difficult industries to work in, so improving skills outside your art form could be a good strategy for achieving success within it. Knowing how to promote yourself is a skill that every artist needs to master.

One example of this may be the painters who promote themselves on social media. By doing this, they will most certainly attract more international attention, which is very likely to help them sell their work to international buyers. Meanwhile, writers who publish articles in well-known newspapers make themselves more visible and could see a significant increase in their book sales, whereas musicians can consider putting on an eye-catching concert with dancers rather than appearing alone on stage.

In the world of art, it is important to realise that artistic skills alone might not be enough to guarantee success. Self-promotion is equally important!

Check!

1 **Read the text above and underline the modal verbs and phrases that express possibility.**

Notice

2 **Which two examples from Exercise 1 express a very high level of possibility?**

....

Focus

3 Circle the correct options.

With the popularity of online streaming music platforms, it *maybe / may be*[1] difficult for musicians to sell physical copies of their music, like CDs and records. As the streaming platforms pay the musicians very little, relying only on them to make money *could / might*[2] not be wise. As a result, musicians *is possible / might*[3] have to look elsewhere for their income. For example, nowadays, if you are a musician, it is *very possibly / very likely*[4] that you make most of your money by giving concerts and going on tour, but this is not necessarily a bad thing as it *possibly / can*[5] generate a lot more money than it used to and *will certainly / will certain*[6] help to raise your profile.

Practice

4 Correct the word order in the sentences below.

a With dedication and practice, you will improve certainly your drawing skills and create beautiful art.

b If you're interested in music, it very likely is that you will end up wanting to play an instrument or write your own songs.

c Certainly exploring various art forms and styles will broaden your artistic understanding and inspire new ideas for your work.

d It highly likely seems that the newspaper review will help to promote his show.

Challenge

5 Write ideas in your notebook of the kind of problems an actor might have when looking for work and possible solutions. Then write a short email to a friend who is trying to find acting work and has asked for your advice.

GET IT RIGHT!

When expressing possibility with the words *certainly* and *likely*, pay close attention to the word order and which words are used to add emphasis.

When used with *will*, the word *certainly* is placed before or after the modal verb but cannot be placed after the second verb. The word most can be used to add emphasis.

Examples:

The book review will (most) certainly help to promote your work. ✓

The book review (most) certainly will help to promote your work. ✓

The book review will help certainly to promote your work. ✗

Likely is placed after the verb. The words *very* and *highly* can be placed before *likely* to add emphasis.

Examples:

It seems (very) likely that the dance will be cancelled. ✓

It likely seems that the dance will be cancelled. ✗

Use of English: The passive

USE OF ENGLISH

Art is not only made for decoration

It is sometimes argued that art's only function is decorative. However, this is a rather simplistic view. It is well documented that our emotions can be altered by artwork. That said, our emotions may not always be affected in positive ways. Artwork is often created as a response to social problems and the viewer may be forced to reflect on issues that are uncomfortable or upsetting. Many artists prefer to be known for the message behind their art rather than its beauty. They simply want to be heard. They choose art as their means of communication and have little intention of creating something decorative.

Check!

1 **Read the text above. Underline the uses of the passive.**

Notice

2 **Match one example from Exercise 1 with each type of passive.**

- a 'It' sentence with the passive ....
- b passive infinitive form ....
- c modal verb and passive ....

3 **Match the beginning (a–c) to the correct ending (i–iii) of each grammar rule. Use the examples from Exercise 2 to help you, if needed.**

- a In 'it' sentences with the passive
- b In infinitive passive structures
- c In modal passive structures

- i the word 'be' is used without 'to'.
- ii the verb 'to be' is written in the infinitive form and follows the sentence's main verb.
- iii the verb 'to be' is written in a past, present, perfect or future form.

Focus

4 Correct the mistake in each sentence.

a It is widely believe that great art is a result of hard work over many years, as opposed to chance.

b Thanks to advances in technology, high quality music tracks can been recorded at home.

c I would like be known for painting interesting and unique pieces of art.

d Many actors don't want to being recognised when they are out on the street.

Practice

5 Rewrite the underlined part of the sentences using the passive 'it' structure.

a <u>People often say</u> that art should make the viewer think.

....

b <u>People generally think</u> that artists and musicians are born talented, but it actually requires hours and hours of hard work to become talented.

....

c There are many theories, but <u>no one fully understands</u> why the play wasn't a success. ....

d <u>Many people believe</u> that the best age to start learning an instrument is when you are young. ....

Challenge

6 Use passives and a range of verbs from the Language tip box to express five common opinions about the arts.

a ....

b ....

c ....

d ....

e ....

GET IT RIGHT!

Remember that all passives use the past participle after the verb *to be*. The present participle and the past simple are never used in the passive.

Example:
The music was written and recorded in his bedroom. (not *writing and recording* or *was wrote*)

Remember that the passive is used when it is not important to know who did the action. Use the preposition *by* if the agent of the verb is mentioned.

Example:
It's widely acknowledged (by art historians) *that Leonardo da Vinci produced his paintings in a workshop with many employees.*

LANGUAGE TIP

When referring to opinions, you can use a range of verbs to describe what people think, such as: *believe, claim, assume, acknowledge, say, argue.*

Improve your writing: An opinion essay

1 **In your notebook, write down reasons for and against offering primary school children free musical instrument lessons.**

2 **Read all your ideas again and answer these questions.**

a Would you be in favour of free musical instrument classes in primary schools?

....

b What are the two strongest reasons for your opinion?

....

....

3 **Read topic sentences A–D, which are taken from the model essay on the next page. Then answer these questions.**

a What value does the writer place on learning music in school?

....

b Does the writer support the idea of free musical instrument classes in school?

....

A Current music classes put children off music, often for life, and an important learning opportunity is missed.

B As they are taught at the moment, school music lessons offer a limited and often negative musical and learning experience.

C Cost is often a barrier for families with lower incomes, so by paying for both the instruments and the lessons the government can help.

D In conclusion, there are many reasons why musical instrument lessons should be offered free of charge in primary schools.

4 **Read the model essay. Which paragraph does each of the topic sentences from Exercise 2 belong with? Write the correct letter. Are any of your ideas from Exercise 1 mentioned in the essay?**

1 ☐ Money is often a reason for this, but it means that children never benefit from the experience of putting their knowledge into practice. To address this problem, the question has been raised as to whether primary school children should be offered free musical instrument lessons.

2 ☐ Free classes would provide students with the opportunity to try different instruments before families decide to take on the cost of buying an instrument and paying for music lessons after primary school. For schools, it is not a matter of buying every student that asks for an electric guitar an electric guitar but rather investing in a set of different decent instruments that can be passed on from student to student.

3 ☐ Group classes with cheap, easy-to-learn instruments like recorders or xylophones, while being accessible to all, are often uninspiring. When children are forced to play together on the same instrument, they do not experience how music really works. Basic and general musical theory serves so that one instrument can work together with another. These children never understand the value of the theory they are being taught because they never see it in practice. Furthermore, when students play in a mixed group and on an instrument they enjoy, they develop skills for life. They learn to apply a theory in practice and the importance and challenges of working in a team.

4 ☐ They would remove barriers and offer students a more realistic and enjoyable musical experience. Music is an extremely important learning and social tool, so children must be given all the chances possible to properly decide whether it is something they want to continue learning.

5 **Read the essay question below. Plan your answer in your notebook with two strong reasons to support your opinion. Use the topic sentences from Exercise 3 as a model to help you write your own topic sentences.**

> Music should only be offered as an afterschool activity, rather than a lesson taught during the school day.
> Do you agree or disagree?

WRITING TIP

When you are planning your essay, you can use topic sentences to help you structure and organise your essay.

6 **In your notebook, use your topic sentences from Exercise 5 to write an opinion essay to answer the essay question.**

Check your progress

Vocabulary

1 **Complete the sentences with words from the box.**

conductor	live audience
rhythm	zoom in

a If you .... on an abstract painting, you may be surprised by the details that you didn't notice from further away.

b A .... leads the orchestra and guides the musicians to create one unique sound.

c A .... adds an extra layer of excitement and energy to any performance, creating a special connection between the artist and their fans.

d .... is an essential element of music and dance, setting the pace and creating a sense of movement.

Grammar

2 **Match the beginning of sentences a–d with the correct ending (i–iv).**

a When dancers have proper technique, the number of serious injuries

b If you organise an art show for your paintings, I'm sure at least one or two of your pieces

c Signing a deal with this publisher

d Knowing how to promote your work

i can be as important as your artistic skills in the world of art.

ii could really promote your novel in a way it deserves!

iii will certainly be reduced.

iv will be sold.

Reading

3 **Read the text. Which paragraph does each of the topic sentences A–C belong with? Write the correct letter.**

A As has been mentioned, music offers much more than simply the music itself.

B Music has always been a powerful tool.

C Many people benefit from music, not just those who listen to it.

1 ☐ It can have a positive effect on a person's mood and overall wellbeing. It has been proven that music can improve mental health and can help people cope with symptoms of depression and anxiety. In fact, studies show that listening to music can even increase the production of endorphins and have a positive effect on people's response to pain.

2 ☐ For those who compose and perform there are benefits too. They may be pleased to hear that it helps to stimulate the brain and increases intelligence. Furthermore, performers should remember that even though performing music in front of a live audience can be extremely stressful, it can also be a hugely satisfying experience and help to boost self-confidence. For performers, it's important to keep in mind that mistakes can happen, but that even with minor mistakes, music can still connect people and create a strong feeling of togetherness and community.

3 ☐ Whether it's by composing instrumental music, playing anthems in a brass band or singing lullabies, anyone can experience the joys and benefits of music and use it either to connect more deeply with themselves or with the community around them.

4 **Read the text in Exercise 3 again and think of a suitable title.**

....

Writing

5 **Read the statement below and the students' comments. Do you agree or disagree with the statement? Write an opinion essay of about 200 words in your notebook. Include two or three arguments to support your opinion. You can use one of the comments to support your opinion if you wish.**

Famous artists and musicians are paid too much.

It's unfair that there are untalented artists and musicians who are rich and famous, while many who are talented but not famous struggle to earn money from their art.

If they are rich, it's because they are the best and they deserve it.

REFLECTION

Write answers to these questions in your notebook.

a Are the arts given enough importance in your school? Explain your answer.

b Has anything in this unit made you think of the arts from a different perspective? If so, what?

c Name three ways the arts benefit society.

d Give an example of why a writer may choose to use verbs in the passive form.

e What is the function of topic sentences in academic writing?

5 Journeys

Think about it: Amazing migrations

1 **Read the information below about three different migratory animals. Which of the migrations would you most like to see?**

The Saiga antelope is famous for three things: its rather unusual appearance, its long migration and, unfortunately, its status as an **endangered** species. A **native species** of the steppe lands in Kazakhstan, Uzbekistan, Mongolia and parts of Russia, the antelope migrate north in the summer so the females can give birth to their **calves** in favourable conditions. There is a rich food supply, in part because they eat **toxic plants** that other animals will not eat, so the calves are able to **gain fat** and strength. Then they are ready to accompany their mothers in the mass migration in late autumn when the herds join together and move south to avoid the harsh northern winters.

Whales are an interesting animal when it comes to migration because there are some whale species that migrate while others do not. For those that do migrate, the reasons for migrations are similar to those of **land mammals**. The most common reason is to find food, but others also migrate to reproduce. Migratory whales can be further split into groups. There are those that follow fixed migratory paths, swimming north at specific times of the year and then **retracing the route** and travelling south again later in the year. Others, however, will migrate to a specific area to reproduce, but once the season has finished they will simply head off in whichever direction they please.

In recent years, thousands of Swainson hawks have altered their migration path, temporarily leaving their traditional route along **coastal areas** of California and flying inland to Anza-Borrego Desert State Park. Their reason for flying inland is the huge number of hawk moth larvae that can be found in the desert at the exact time of year the hawks themselves are migrating along routes close by. Scientists have linked the number of hawk moth **caterpillars** each spring to the amount of rainfall. In years of drought, caterpillar numbers have been low and it was not common to see the hawks in the park, but recent years have seen higher rainfall. This has led to more caterpillars and the arrival of more hawks. It is unlikely to become a permanent feature on the hawks' migratory map, but if there have been spring rains you can expect to see them in their thousands, probably with fat, juicy larvae in their **beaks**!

2 Match descriptions a–d with the correct animal from Exercise 1. One animal is described twice.

a They make a stopover on their journey if the weather has been wet.

....

b You may find them feeding in the grassy plains. ....

c They like to visit an area where a specific type of bug lays its eggs.

....

d Some species do not travel the same path in the reverse direction and go back to the place they came from. ....

3 Match the words in bold in Exercise 1 to the definitions below.

a the mouths of birds ....

b long, small animals that develop into butterflies or moths ....

c animals that live on land, rather than in water, and feed their babies milk ....

d go back the way they came ....

e land situated along the ocean or sea ....

f poisonous vegetation ....

g put on weight ....

h so few in number that there is a risk they may soon not exist ....

i the young and babies of animals like cows, antelopes, whales ....

j types of animals that naturally live in an area ....

Challenge

4 Research an endangered migratory animal. Copy and complete the table below in your notebook.

Name	Time of migration	Best place to visit to see the migration	Reason it is endangered

Geography: Reclaiming the migration routes of the shepherds from long ago

1 **Why might farmers move their animals long distances from one area to another? Write your ideas in your notebook. Then read the article. Are any of your ideas mentioned?**

Today the residents of Madrid experienced one of the most spectacular and unlikely sights on the autumn calendar; namely, thousands of sheep being herded through the busiest streets in the Spanish capital. Modern city life came to a halt and witnessed one of the best examples of ancient customs providing solutions to contemporary problems.

Transhumance refers to moving thousands of animals seasonally long distances along well-established paths to areas with a better natural food supply and with more favourable weather conditions. Traditionally, animals were moved on foot, in journeys that could take over a month. Practices changed and farmers preferred to move their animals by truck or to simply keep them in one place and supplement the animals' diet with artificial products. However, the more intense summer heat and the greater frequency of severe droughts in the south of the country and rising costs have forced them to reconsider transhumance.

Environmentalists have praised this move. Not only does this custom help to reduce overgrazing, allowing the plants time to grow back before they are totally destroyed, but it also helps to sustain a healthier environment along the paths. The animals eat the plants along the route, stimulating new plant growth by spreading seeds and naturally fertilising the soil. Moreover, the sheep help to reduce the risk of wildfires by eating the material that causes fires to spread quickly.

Despite all the environmental benefits, the shepherds encounter many challenges along the way, so it is not an easy decision to make. The ancient routes have been neglected and it can be difficult to water the animals and to shelter them from bad weather. It is a unique way of making a living and is certainly not for everyone, but fortunately, as people realise it offers one of the most sustainable ways of producing food, more sheep farmers are choosing it and more consumers and politicians are supporting it.

It is a tradition we need more than we probably realise. So let's step aside and make way for the sheep and the shepherds reclaiming the traditions and wisdom of our ancestors.

2 **Read the text again. Then read these statements and write True, False or Not given.**

a The residents of Madrid were annoyed that the sheep interrupted their busy day. ....

b The animals are moved whenever the weather gets unpleasant for them. ....

c Some farmers find other ways to overcome the lack of natural food. ....

d Economic factors cause some farmers to make the journey on foot. ....

e The sheep overgraze the paths and destroy the plants. ....

f Being a shepherd is a sustainable way to live. ....

g It is not always easy to protect the animals from harsh conditions along the way. ....

3 **In your own words, explain why the text mentions the following:**

a wildfires ....

b environmentalists ....

c ancestors ....

4 **What do you think the writer means when they say 'It is a tradition we need more than we probably realise'?**

....

5 **Read the text again. What problems might there be if the sheep do not make this journey?**

....

Challenge

6 **Carry out some research on other countries where transhumance farming is practised and write a list in your notebook.**

Use of English: Superlative forms

USE OF ENGLISH

Hey fellow travellers!

Today, I'm writing about the two-day train trip I took from Vancouver to Jasper in Canada. I think this train ride might have been my best one yet! Not only was it the fanciest train ride I've been on, with the best food ever, but it was also the most memorable. Everything is designed to give you the most amazing views possible, including the biggest windows you can imagine on a train, a glass ceiling and even an outside viewing platform. It was a real luxury because the landscape was unbelievably beautiful! We travelled alongside rivers, through breathtaking canyons and up into the highest mountains in the Canadian Rockies. Truly unforgettable!

Check!

1 **Read the travel blog entry above.**
Underline all the examples of the superlative form.

2 **Give one example from the blog that…**

a uses *the* + *-est* ....

b uses the *most* ....

c changes *y* to an *i* ....

d doubles the consonant ....

e has an irregular superlative form ....

Notice

3 **Read the blog again. Circle the correct option in the sentences below.**

a For the superlative form of one-syllable words and some two-syllable words, use *the + -est / the most.*

b For the superlative form of some two-syllable words and all words of three or more syllables, use *the + -est / the most.*

Focus

4 Correct the mistakes. Two sentences are correct.

a I didn't want my bag to weigh too much so I packed the thinest jacket I had.

b That is the heavyest suitcase I have ever seen! How are you going to carry it?

c It's not a good idea to visit in October – it's the wettest month of the year.

d We were very unlucky; the day we went up the Eiffel Tower it was the greyest day of our holiday, and we couldn't see much from the top.

e August is one of the busyest times of the year so plane tickets are expensive.

Practice

5 Complete the sentences using the superlative form of the adjectives in the box.

far good practical quiet spicy

a I love to travel, but sometimes .... part of travelling is arriving back home.

b .... food I ever tried was in India – I couldn't stop sweating!

c Some airports no longer announce their flights; these so-called 'silent' airports aim to be .... in the world.

d In remote areas, generally, ... way to travel is renting a car.

e .... I've ever travelled is to Chile in South America.

Challenge

6 Complete the beginning of the sentences below with the superlative forms of the adjectives from the box. Then complete the sentences by writing about your own travel experiences.

boring enjoyable long

a The .... journey I ever had was ....

b The .... journey I ever had was ....

c The .... journey I ever had was ....

GET IT RIGHT!

Remember that we double the consonant in adjectives where the last three letters are consonant, vowel, consonant (CVC words), such as *hot* and *thin*.

Example:
We travelled on the ***hottest*** *day of the year, it was terrible.*

Remember we change *y* to *i* when the letter before the *y* is a consonant, as in *dry*, but not when the letter before the *y* is a vowel, as in *grey*.

Example:
We can't grow anything here – it's the ***driest, greyest*** *soil I've ever seen!*

Use of English: Past simple, past continuous and past perfect simple used in storytelling

USE OF ENGLISH

Last summer, I **went** away for a long weekend with my family. We **had planned** a trip to the countryside. We **woke up** bright and early, ready to catch the train, and everyone **was feeling** excited, but things **didn't go** as planned. As we **were walking** to the station, I **noticed** my pocket **was** empty, Oh no! I **had forgotten** my phone. I **rushed** back to the house to get it. When I eventually **arrived** at the station, my family **were waiting** for me on the platform and they **looked** so disappointed – the train **had left**. Definitely not a great way to start the weekend!

Check!

1 **Read the text. Then look at the examples in bold and write one example next to each of these verb forms.**

a past simple ....

b past continuous ....

c past perfect simple ....

2 **Read the text again. Complete the information.**

In storytelling we use the…

a .... to describe actions or events that happened before the events in the story.

b .... to say what happened, often the short actions told in the order that they happened.

c .... to describe a longer action, often interrupted by another action.

Notice

3 **Which verb form is used in storytelling to set the scene of the story?**

....

Focus

4 Circle the correct past forms.

I *heard / had heard*[1] about how marvellous Paris was, but as I came out of the station I *wondered / had wondered*[2] if it really was going to be so special. Cars *were rushing / had rushed*[3] by and no one *was smiling / had smiled*[4]. I lived in a small town and I *was never seeing / had never seen*[5] the bright lights and busy streets of a big city, so it *felt / was feeling*[6] strange and lonely. Although I *had / was having*[7] friends in Paris, I *had not made / was not making*[8] any plans to meet them. I *wanted / was wanting*[9] to walk the streets alone first. I *was buying / had bought*[10] a new camera and I needed time to myself to take some pictures.

Practice

5 Read the sentences and correct the mistakes.

a It was a boring train ride. Outside it ~~rained~~ was raining, and raindrops were running down the window. The only thing I had to do was watch them.

b I arrived at the café on time and my friend was waiting for me. Two coffees were sitting on the table and she was smiling; she was looking so happy. I could tell she had good news.

c As I walked through the park, the birds were singing, the flowers bloomed and the sun was shining. Spring had arrived.

d I opened the front door to find my sister was screaming, my brother was running after her with a spider, Mum was singing in the kitchen and the air was smelling of coffee. I knew I was home.

Challenge

6 In your notebook, write a short text about a travel experience you have had. Try to include a range of forms for expressing what happened in the past.

GET IT RIGHT!

When telling a story, we use the past continuous to set the scene, not the past simple.

Example:
When I found my seat, a baby ***was crying*** *in the row behind and some teenagers* ***were chatting and laughing*** *in the row in front.*

Remember that stative verbs are not normally written in the continuous form.

Example:
It ***looked*** *like chaos. So I put my headphones on and went to sleep.*

Improve your writing: Descriptive writing

1 **Circle the best words to make the text more descriptive and interesting.**

My journey to the top in the rock-climbing world started early. You see, I grew up with rock-climbing parents and have been messing around on rocks since I was *small* / *tiny*[1]. When I was about 12 years old, I started dreaming of being a *really good* / *world-class*[2] rock-climber and I've never looked back. It may sound *incredibly* / *very* strange[3] to you, but hanging on the end of a rope actually felt *very* / *totally*[4] natural to me. Of course, that's because I was *very good* / *extremely strict*[5] about safety – my parents had taught me that. I make sure I have *good* / *top-quality*[6] equipment. I also train *tremendously* / *very*[7] hard away from the rock face to keep up my strength and my flexibility.

2 **Read the text in Exercise 1 again.**
Which of these techniques for writing a descriptive text did the writer use?

A describe feelings and sensations ☐

B describe what they have learnt from the experience ☐

C talk directly to the reader ☐

D include his thoughts ☐

WRITING TIP

Remember that addressing the reader directly is a powerful way to interest the reader. However, it makes the text more informal and is not suitable for formal academic texts like reports or essays. It can be used in creative and descriptive writing.

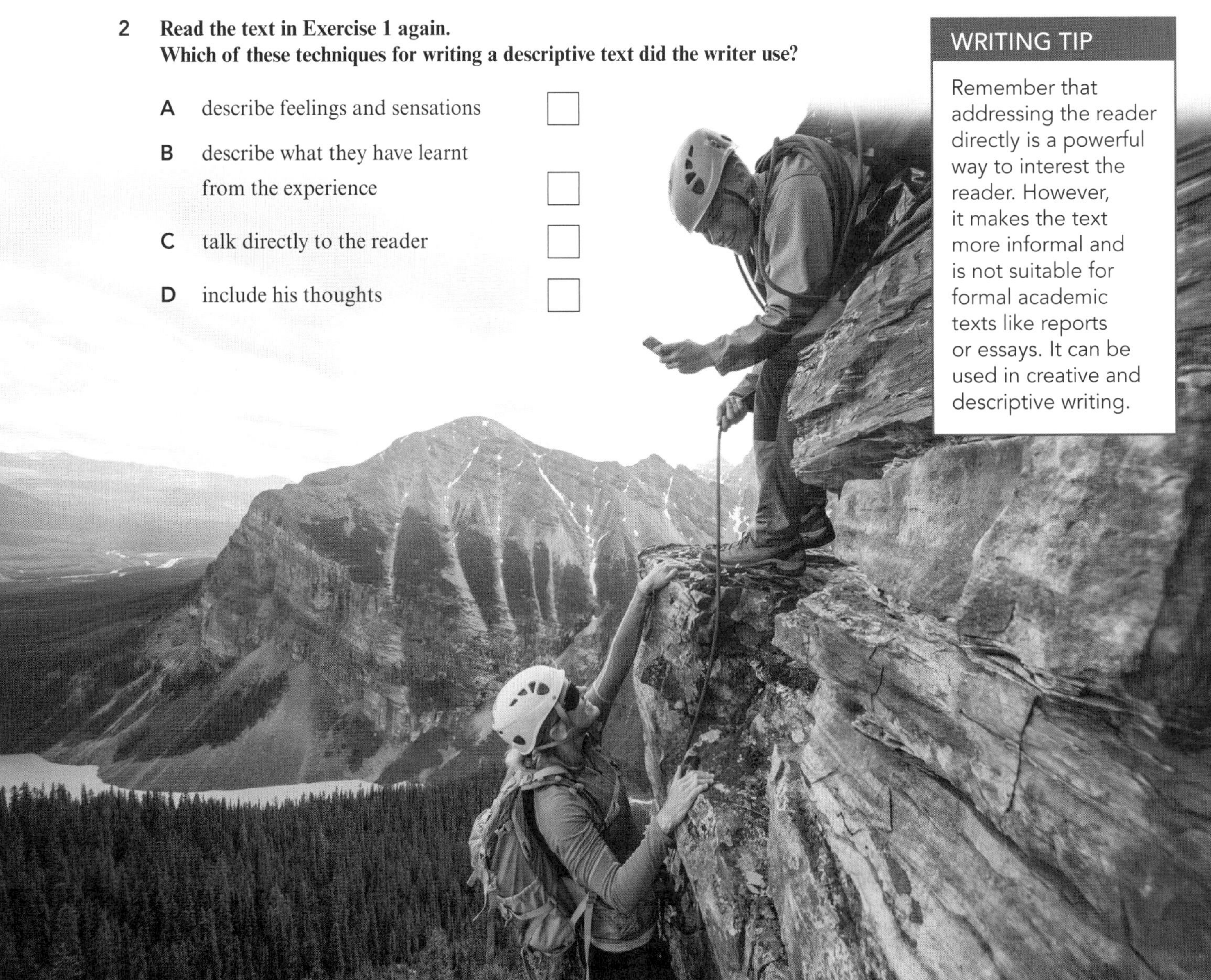

3 **Complete the graphic organiser with the ideas 1–8 from the box.**

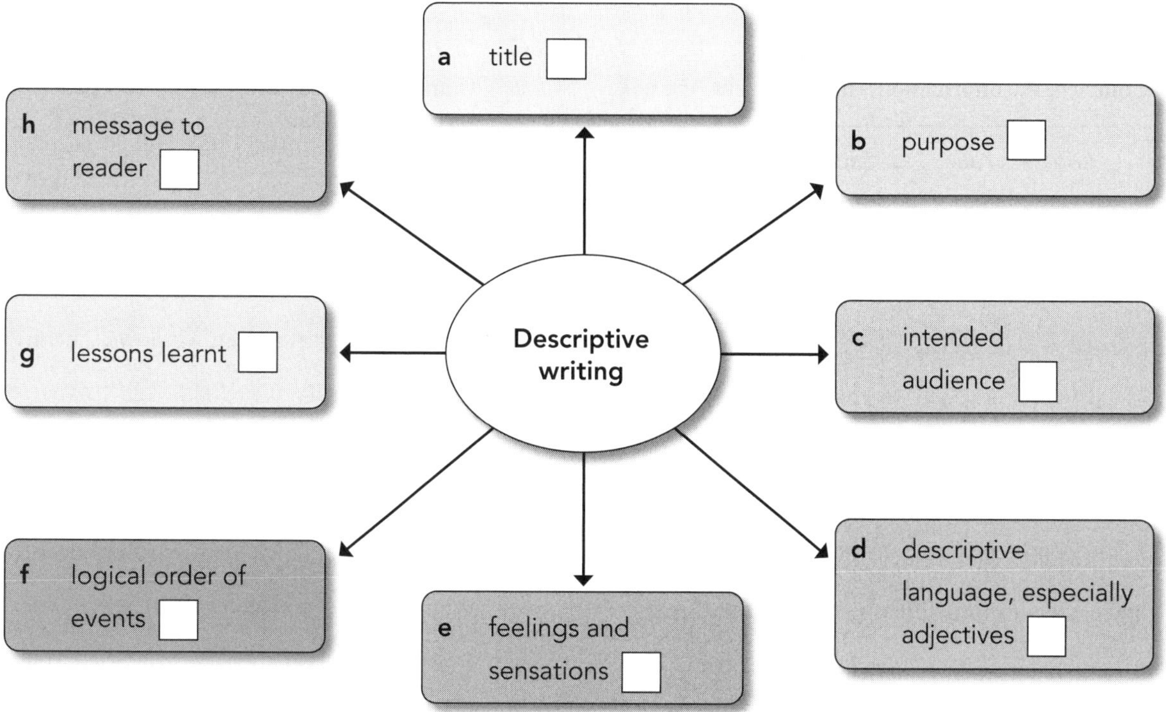

1 challenging, extremely rewarding, fantastic teaching skills, unlimited support
2 don't give up, find people to support you
3 Dreams can come true!
4 early years no experience, changed trainers, now feel supported
5 intense pain in my leg, I wanted to give up, 'I can do this'
6 My journey to the top
7 people my age (informal language)
8 to entertain and motivate the reader

4 **Read the task. In your notebook, use a graphic organiser to plan your answer, then write your descriptive text.**

> Write a blog entry about something you worked hard to achieve and the 'journey' you had while preparing yourself.

Check your progress

Vocabulary

1 Complete the information with words from the box.

coastal areas	endangered	gain fat
grassy plains	land mammals	lay eggs

Many migratory animals are ....[1] because it is no longer easy for them to make their journeys. Train tracks and highways cut through the ....[2], adding new dangers to the migration journey many ....[3] face. Meanwhile, beach resorts in ....[4] have made it more difficult for migratory birds to ....[5] and to find food and ....[6], which they need to make the long journey home.

Grammar

2 Complete the text using the correct past forms of the verbs in brackets.

At the airport, I ....[1] (got) a taxi to the hotel. Music ....[2] (play) on the radio and a warm breeze ....[3] (blow) through the open windows. The driver was surprised that I ....[4] (never go) to Morocco before. He ....[5] (tell) me funny stories about some of the other tourists he ....[6] (drive) around over the years. At a traffic light, some women ....[7] (sell) flowers. He ....[8] (buy) two bouquets and gave one to me. 'Welcome to Morocco,' he said, then explained the other was for his daughter because she ....[9] (just have) a baby! It was a nice surprise and such an entertaining taxi ride!

Reading

3 **Read the travel blog. Then read the statements and write True, False or Not given.**

The best part of my holiday was definitely the ride in a hot air balloon. Mum and I joined some other tourists really early in the morning for the flight. We had received a confirmation email with the precise departure details and useful instructions to take warm clothes and to wear appropriate footwear, which was good because we were standing in the middle of a wet field at 5 o'clock in the morning!

The pilot explained that the hours around sunrise and sunset are the best times to fly, not because they are the most beautiful but because it's when the air currents are the most predictable. At these times, pilots can more or less plan the route, although they can never be completely sure of the destination; that depends on the wind. Before we took off, the pilot went through some safety rules, which helped to calm our nerves and assure us that we were in good hands.

We watched eagerly as the crew got the balloon ready. There was a lot of noise from the gas burner and I was worried it was going to be like that the whole journey, but it wasn't. Once we were all aboard, the balloon started to rise and we were soon high above the trees. Then the pilot cut the burner and we were just silently floating in the air. It was truly magical and a most memorable way to start the day. I would definitely recommend it, as long as you've got a head for heights of course!

a The writer was glad that they had been told what shoes to wear. ....

b Hot air balloon journeys take place in the morning and evening because they are the prettiest times of the day.

....

c The pilot knew exactly where our take-off and landing points would be. ....

d The pilot prepared the balloon on her own.

....

e The writer hadn't expected the balloon to be so noisy. ....

4 **Answer these questions in your own words about the text in Exercise 3.**

a How did the writer feel after they heard the pilot's instructions?

....

b Who does the writer say should go on a hot air balloon ride?

....

Writing

5 **In your notebook, write a short description about a memorable journey you have had.**

REFLECTION

Write answers to these questions in your notebook.

a How can humans help migratory animals?

b What are the benefits of taking the transhumance sheep through the centre of Madrid?

c Our ideal travel destinations are often the biggest, best or most beautiful places. What problems might this cause?

d Most of us are constantly on the move. List five benefits of spending more time at home.

e In what ways is writing a descriptive text different from writing other texts?

6 Making a change

Think about it: Living with smart technology

1 **Complete the responses to a survey about modern technology. Use words from the box.**

access to	reliable wi-fi connection	screen time	smart technology	social media account

A These days most adults and teenagers have at least one ....[1], if not more. Given that these are designed to keep you connected to them throughout the day, most people have more ....[2] each day than they realise. Even for those who do not suffer from online related FOMO and peer pressure, we all definitely need to take a break sometimes and live in the real world.

B Sending data to be stored on the internet through a storage provider saves space on your computer. Even though this makes it accessible from anywhere, it also requires a ....[3], which may be a problem if you are travelling.

C It would help a lot if governments invested in schools and public libraries, and offered courses to ensure that everyone, young, old, rich or poor have ....[4] the same ....[5] that, at the moment, only wealthy young people can use.

2 **Match each of these questions to the correct response (A–C) from Exercise 1.**

a What can be done to achieve **digital equality** for every section of society? ☐

b How seriously should we consider going on a **digital detox**? ☐

c Are there any disadvantages of **storing data in the cloud**? ☐

3 **Tick the correct word that matches the definition.**

a When a device or the screen on a device stops responding and keeps the same image, even though the image should go away or change.

☐ block ☐ jam ☐ freeze

b A smooth surface on a device that shows information and pictures and is controlled by touching it rather than by buttons or a keyboard.

☐ window ☐ pad ☐ touchscreen

c The action of changing the size and dimensions of a digital image.

☐ cut a photo ☐ crop a photo ☐ rearrange a photo

d An environment created by a computer that feels real to the viewer and that the viewer can participate in and control.

☐ alternate world ☐ digital reality ☐ virtual reality

e A virtual image or character that is used by different users of a program or website to represent themselves, which the user can control, move around and use to interact with other users.

☐ avatar ☐ cartoon ☐ profile

Challenge

4 **Fill in the table with information about yourself.**

Number of social media accounts	
Number of smart technology devices	
Hours of screentime each day	
Frequency of digital detox	
Type of information stored in the cloud	

5 **Write about your own experience of one of the concepts written in bold in Exercise 2 using some of the information included in the table in Exercise 4. Write a paragraph in your notebook.**

Technology: Studying technology

1 **Read the article below. What is the author's opinion of technology in schools? Do you agree?**

....

....

Technology plays a greater role in our daily life as every day goes by. We are at a point where it is nearly impossible to think of a work environment that does not require the use of some kind of technological device. For this reason, schools must now reconsider the value of technology classes in the school curriculum. Traditionally, technology has not been considered a **core subject**, but it is most certainly time to **grant** it this **status**.

There is no doubt that technological equipment can be very expensive, so the introduction of technology as a core subject would require significant financial investment. This is not an insignificant barrier. However, schools that are reluctant must remember that one of the primary roles of the education system is to prepare students for the workplace.

Years ago, being good at technology was regarded as being able to manage the basic functions of a computer. These days, proper technical **competence** demands in-depth knowledge of a number of different programs and **mastery** of a wide range of technological devices. Places of education must adapt to the requirements of the labour market and ensure that students are fully **computer literate** when they graduate from compulsory school. Furthermore, schools must also invest in teacher training so that all subjects have technology incorporated into their daily activities, in much the same way that other workplaces do.

The digital revolution started decades ago. It is time for schools to wake up and get with the programme. Students should expect, or maybe demand, to see a lot more technology on their timetables!

core subject: the most important subjects in the school curriculum that all students must study, often the students' native language, maths and English

grant: to give something officially

status: amount of respect or importance given to something

competence: ability to do something well

mastery: sufficient skills to be in complete control of a situation or subject

computer literate: able to use computers well

2 **Read the text again and answer these questions.**

a What is the main purpose of the text?

....

b Give two reasons why schools may be unwilling to offer more technology classes in school.

....

....

c What do you think the writer means by 'digital revolution' in the final paragraph?

....

3 **Read the final paragraph again.**
Tick the correct meaning of the idiom 'get with the programme'.

A to use as much digital technology as possible ☐

B to accept new ideas and ways of doing things ☐

C to organise a series of events to raise money ☐

4 **Why do you think the author chose to use the idiom 'get with the programme'? Is the author writing in British English or American English?**

....

Challenge

5 **How much technology is offered and used in your school? In your notebook, make one list of what is currently offered and used in your school and another list of what else you think should be offered or used.**

....

....

....

....

....

....

....

....

....

LANGUAGE TIP

In British English there is a difference between *program* and *programme*.

Program refers to the series of instructions that a computer uses to perform a function.

Example:
*The computer **program** is very old; it needs to be updated.*

Programme refers to something that is broadcast on TV or radio, or a series of organised activities or events.

Example:
*I watched my favourite TV **programme** last night.*

*My school offers a special arts **programme** that is not available in many other schools.*

In American English, the word *program* is used for all of these meanings.

Use of English: Expressing probability and certainty

USE OF ENGLISH

Even though we know that we own devices which use smart technology, **the chances are** not everybody could explain what makes them 'smart'. Smart devices are those that interact with other devices or networks. If you were asked to name a smart device, you would **most likely** name a smart phone or a smart TV, but the group can also include fridges, lights, speakers and even doorbells. Any household equipment that has a Wi-Fi or Bluetooth option can be called a smart device. However, with the appearance of artificial intelligence (AI), we **may well** have to think of a new word for them, as it is AI devices that **will** truly think for themselves, or in other words, be 'smart'.

Check!

1 **Read the text. Write the words in bold next to the correct term.**

probability ....

certainty ....

Notice

2 **Tick the sentences below that express a high level of certainty. Then add the words next to the correct term in Exercise 1.**

a They can't be more intelligent than humans; they are only machines, after all. ☐

b Some people worry that perhaps all this smart technology will make humans less intelligent. ☐

c It's clear that smart technology has changed the way we live. ☐

d The neighbours must control their house remotely; lights go on, curtains open and close, but we never see anyone there. ☐

Focus

3 **Complete the sentences with words from the box. In some sentences, more than one option may be possible. Use each word or phrase in the box once.**

can't	It's clear	may well	most likely	the chances are	will

a If your device was bought recently, ... it has an energy-saving design.

b It's a more expensive model so it .... have smart features that the cheaper model doesn't have.

c If you have smart devices, you will .... be able to control them remotely.

d Having smart devices at home .... make living alone for older people a lot easier.

e .... that AI is the most important technological advance in recent years.

f That child .... be using a smartphone – she's far too young!

Practice

4 **Rewrite these sentences using *certainly* or *surely*. The word order of the sentence may need to be changed.**

a The device does have a safety feature, doesn't it, to protect the user's privacy?

....

b There has to be a wi-fi signal, right?

....

c There's no doubt that smart locks have made life easier for those of us who can never find our keys.

....

d As online shopping becomes more popular, drones will be used for a higher percentage of the transport, for sure.

....

Challenge

5 **What impact do you think technology will have on schools in the next 20 years? Write your ideas in your notebook. Use at least five different ways of expressing probability and certainty.**

GET IT RIGHT!

Be careful not to confuse the meaning of *certainly* and *surely*. We use *certainly* to show we have no doubts about something. We use *surely* to express a lower level of certainty together with a desire for someone to confirm our opinion.

Examples:

Staying in touch with family is ***certainly*** *easier now that we have smartphones.* (I have no doubt about this.)

Staying in touch with family is ***surely*** *easier now that we have smartphones.* (I think it should be but I would like someone to agree with me.)

Use of English: Linking words and phrases (contrast and addition)

USE OF ENGLISH

Robots working for us around the house is closer and closer to being a reality. **However**, the thought of living with machines that can think for themselves raises questions, and not everyone is convinced it is progress. **Despite** the fact that these devices are designed to make tasks easier and quicker, some people worry about possible negative impacts on our health or relationships. These concerns are valid, **yet** many people's lives would indeed improve. For people with limited mobility, for example, it could give them the independence they need to live on their own. **As well as** this, robots could also free up parents from housework and give them more time to spend with their children. **Furthermore**, we wouldn't have to argue anymore about whose turn it was to take out the rubbish or unload the dishwasher. Over all, **although** there will certainly be some negative impacts, it is important to consider the opportunities robots will also provide.

Check!

1 **Read text and answer these questions.**

Which linking words are used to:

a contrast information? ....

b give additional information? ....

Notice

2 **Complete the information below with words from the box.**

as well as	clause	comma	despite	previous

a Sentences with linking words often contain a ...., which helps to separate the information being linked.

b *However* and *furthermore* are used to link information in one sentence with information in the .... sentence.

c Some linking words, for example .... and ...., are followed by a noun or noun phrase.

d Linking words such as *even though* and *yet* cannot be followed only by a noun or noun phrase; they are followed by a ....

Focus

3 The following sentences contain the wrong linking words. Correct the linking words. Use the words in bold from Exercise 1 to help you.

a Despite I hadn't read the news, I found out about the accident on social media.

b My mum has taken my smartphone away from me furthermore my TV.

c I wouldn't mind having a robot to help me clean around the house. Furthermore, I would still like to do the cooking myself.

d I find this social media site takes up too much of my time. As well as, I don't generally enjoy its content.

e Even though my efforts, I can't manage to stay off social media for more than two hours at a time.

GET IT RIGHT!

Check your spelling when using linking words. Some linking words are written as separate words, such as *as well as* (not *aswell as*) and *in spite of* (not *inspite of*), while others are one word made up of shorter words, such as *however* (not *how ever*) and *nevertheless* (not *never the less*).

Examples:
*Robots can help people to be more independent. **Nevertheless**, they can also lead to social isolation and loneliness.*

***In spite of** helping people to be more independent, robots can also lead to social isolation and loneliness.*

Practice

4 Correct the mistakes in the sentences below. One sentence is correct.

a All though smart technology is expensive, schools must be prepared to make this investment.

b I couldn't find the device I need anywhere in town, dispite looking in every single computer shop.

c These days cropping photos to get the perfect social media picture is common. Furthermore, people normally adjust the colours.

d Eventhough it's an easy program to use, it offers loads of possibilities.

e My cousin's school has a fantastic technology department, where as my school doesn't at all.

Challenge

5 Choose one of the following topics. Write a paragraph in your notebook about the present situation and how it may change in the future.

robots in schools | self-drive cars | robots in hospitals

Improve your writing: A discursive essay

1 **Read the list of common mistakes made when writing an essay. Which do you think you are most likely to make?**

The essay…

- doesn't answer the question ☐
- has a poor structure ☐
- describes the question topic rather than analyses it ☐
- uses poor language. ☐

2 **Match the definitions (a–e) of different writing tasks with the correct writing tasks (i–v).**

a	a piece of writing that evaluates how good or bad a film, book, product, etc. is	☐	i	an article
b	a piece of writing that presents and supports the author's opinion	☐	ii	a discursive essay
c	a piece of writing that presents both sides of an argument equally	☐	iii	a review
d	a piece of writing written to entertain the reader	☐	iv	a report
e	a piece of writing that informs the reader of a present situation and suggests improvements	☐	v	a persuasive essay

3 **Read the writing task. Underline the keywords. What type of task is it? Explain your answer in your notebook.**

> Allowing mobile phones in classrooms is a controversial topic. Many people believe students should be allowed to use their phones in class, while others believe it is not helpful to allow phones in classrooms.
>
> Discuss both views equally and give your opinion.

4 **Read the different stages of writing an essay. Put them in the correct order from 1 to 5.**

☐ **Write** – follow the plan as you write, include topic sentences and linking words to help the reader.

☐ **Brainstorm** – think about the topic from different points of view, write them down, include your own point of view.

☐ **Check and correct** – check any changes made in the previous stage flow properly. Focus on the language, check for spelling and punctuation mistakes, improve the vocabulary if necessary.

☐ **Prepare and plan** – decide on the structure, which ideas from the brainstorming to focus on, and what evidence or examples you can use to support your ideas.

☐ **Revise and change** – revise the content and structure, make sure that you have answered the question, that you have the correct structure and that the main points you wanted to make are clear.

5 Look at the photo. How would a teacher versus a student feel about the mobile phones being in the drawer?

Teacher: ....

Student: ....

6 Read the writing task from Exercise 3 again. Circle the signposting expressions below that would be suitable for this kind of task.

A	Another point in favour…	F	I believe that although…
B	Everybody knows…	G	A negative point is…
C	My teacher says…	H	I really like it because…
D	An important advantage is…	I	There are benefits for…
E	The kids in my class think…	J	The majority of students argue that…

7 Plan and write your own answer to the writing task in Exercise 3. Follow the steps described in Exercise 4 and use the appropriate signposting from Exercise 6 where necessary. Write the essay in your notebook.

LANGUAGE TIP

The expression *On the one hand… on the other hand* is often used to contrast two different ideas or opinions. It is useful when presenting both sides of an argument as equally valid.

On the one hand *technology has made it easier for people to stay in touch.* ***On the other hand****, advances in technology make it difficult for people to relax and enjoy the moment.*

On the other hand can be used on its own to present new contrasting information.

Technology has made our lives so much easier in many ways. ***On the other hand****, we have become totally dependent on our devices.*

Check your progress

Vocabulary

1 **Complete the sentences. Use words from the box.**

account	cloud	crop	detox	smart

a She turned off her phone for an entire week in order to get a proper digital ....

b It's a good idea to store data in the .... if you're running out of space on your device.

c In most cases, you have to be over a certain age to have a social media ....

d She renovated her house to replace all her old devices with ones run by .... technology.

e I'll have to .... the photo to remove the person – I don't know who he is.

Grammar

2 **Correct the sentences.**

a I don't think I will buy the next model, it may likely be out of my budget.

b The age at which children receive their first smartphone is well likely to continue falling.

c The chance is that elderly members of your family will need help with their devices as newer versions are released.

d There will certainly be some negative consequences when robots are introduced into our homes. Never the less, it is important to consider all the extra free time families will gain.

e Having smart devices at home can make living alone for older people a lot easier aswell as safer.

Reading

3 **Read the text and answer the questions. Explain each of your answers.**

> Long gone are the days of looking through the pages of a holiday brochure and dreaming about your next holiday in the sun. If you tell young people that the only way to book a flight was by asking a travel agent to call the airline company, they will probably look at you in disbelief. Yet this is actually how it was for many of the older generation. It simply wasn't possible to click a few buttons and book a trip to some faraway place. Furthermore, if you were actually lucky enough to go to a faraway place, the most contact you could expect to have with your family and friends back home was writing a postcard to them. There was no need to think about digital detox holidays because there were no social media accounts to detox from!

a How long ago do you think the writer is talking about?

....

b Do you think that the writer thinks that everything is better now?

....

c Would you have found it easy or difficult to travel in the times described in the text?

....

Writing

4 **Complete the extract from a discursive essay with the correct signposting expressions from the box.**

A major advantage is A major disadvantage of using Another important point is It is certainly there are other points

....[1] true that technology in school helps to prepare students for real life. ....[2] that schools provide an environment where students can be taught how to use technology responsibly. In addition, for the majority of students, technology can help them with their studies.

However, ...[3] to consider. Firstly, students need to be shown that they can study without technology and develop the skills to do so. ....[4] that students need to develop their social skills, and schools can provide the opportunity to do this. ....[5] technology in schools would be the loss of some of these opportunities.

REFLECTION

Write answers to these questions in your notebook.

a Describe three ways that technology has made your family's life easier.

b Do you think a digital detox is necessary? If so, how long and how often?

c To what extent did this unit make you reflect on your own screen time?

d What new linking words or expressions have you learnt in this unit?

e Which of the steps in completing a writing task do you need to improve at doing?

7 Our planet, our home

Think about it: Every little change helps

1 **Read the news article extracts. Match the newspaper headline with the correct extract.**

a **Paving the way towards an environmentally friendly solution to global problem**

b **Voices from the classrooms, but no angry teachers**

c **Charity warns Europe could get a lot colder**

1 Around the world, teenagers united on Friday in a joint **initiative** for Earth Day. Having been given permission to leave their school books in their bags for the day, they instead sat at their desks and wrote emails, signed petitions and raised money all in support of environmental **campaigns** that hope to influence decision-makers, both nationally and globally.

2 Protect the Ocean, a non-profit organisation that aims to raise **awareness** about how the oceans and the global climate are connected, emphasises that changes in **sea currents** may not only cause many marine species to die out but could actually change the climate and lower temperatures in countries such as Ireland, the United Kingdom and even Norway.

3 Nzambi Matee, a young Kenyan engineer and environmentalist, is fighting plastic pollution by turning single-use plastic bottles into building materials. The bricks she produces can be used to make paths and outdoor walkways. Rather than being dumped into landfills or floating in the ocean, the bottles are recycled and given a new purpose.

2 **Read the article extracts again and answer the questions.**

Which article mentions…

a people writing their names on a document to show they want change? ☐

b a product that is designed to be used once then thrown away? ☐

c an establishment that is run like a business but whose main aim is social or environmental rather than financial? ☐

d a place where rubbish is buried? ☐

e the risk of some animals no longer existing? ☐

f damage caused by a specific material? ☐

3 **Match the words in bold from Exercise 1 with the correct meaning.**

a knowledge and understanding of a situation ....

b a planned group of activities intended to lead to a particular change in the behaviour or the opinions of others ....

c the flow of ocean water along a particular path as if it were an underwater river ....

d a new plan for solving a problem or improving a situation ....

Challenge

4 **Write about any changes you have made or would like to make to help protect the planet, such as using more energy-efficient items at home. Write a paragraph.**

....

....

....

....

....

....

....

....

....

....

....

....

Environmental science: An award-winning environmentalist

declaration: an official announcement or decision

1 **The Eco-Hero awards are given to youths who start projects that protect the planet. Read the article about Francisco, who won second place in the Eco-Hero awards in 2022. Fill the gap with the age you think Francisco was when he started his project.**

When he was just .... years old, Francisco Marin from Honduras started a project he called Jum Te Rum, which means 'paper, tree, earth' in the Mayan Chorti language, a native language in Honduras. His aim is to help the environment through reforestation, recycling, and educating and raising awareness among young people about climate change.

Francisco raised enough money from gathering and selling 1000 pounds (approximately 450 kg) of recycled paper to purchase 150 young trees, which were planted in areas damaged by deforestation. He donated additional funds from recycling to a non-profit organisation for the blind.

In Honduras, he explains, climate change issues are not addressed well in the schools. Since his father is an educator, he decided to inspect the school curriculums for first through ninth grades to see how recycling was taught. He created and distributed a questionnaire to 340 teenagers in four schools. It was discovered that the biggest gap in knowledge was on climate change. People have heard about climate change but cannot understand the details of it. Consequently, students do not know how to act in the face of climate change problems.

Francisco is working on a government **declaration** to get curriculums into schools covering the natural sciences and climate change. Furthermore, to raise awareness, he has appeared on television stations and has written articles for the press.

Francisco is converting his project into a network of young people and has already educated 200 students about climate change issues. As he works to get the climate change curriculum into schools, he also hopes to travel outside of Honduras and meet world leaders and decision-makers.

2 **Read the text again. Which of the following statements is Francisco most likely to make?**

A My goal is to raise as much money as possible for a non-profit organisation for the blind. ☐

B My goal is to reduce the effects of climate change through the improvement of the education system. ☐

C My goal is to tell world leaders about the importance of the forest in Honduras. ☐

3 **Circle the correct word to complete these sentences.**

a The *reforestation* / *deforestation* project to bring back the forest was a success, making the environment healthier and more beautiful.

b After the chemicals were accidentally spilled, a specially trained team worked hard to *recontaminate* / *decontaminate* the area and make it safe and clean again.

c The city decided to *reconstruct* / *deconstruct* the old bridge, using new materials and skilled workers to make it strong and safe once more after it was destroyed by flooding.

d To protect endangered animals and stop them from dying out, experts often release young animals back into their natural habitats in an attempt to *repopulate* / *depopulate* those areas.

LANGUAGE TIP

The prefixes *re-* and *de-* can be added to many words, usually nouns or verbs.

Re- means to do something again, for example *reforestation* – the planting of new trees so a forest can grow back.

Example:
His aim is to help the environment through reforestation.

De- means to reduce or remove something, for example *deforestation* – the destruction of a forest through human activity.

Example:
The trees were planted in areas damaged by deforestation.

Challenge

4 **Do some research about another teenager who has won an award for their environmental work. Write a short text about them.**

....

....

....

....

....

....

....

....

....

....

....

Use of English: First and second conditional structures

USE OF ENGLISH

If you drink a lot of lemonade or cola, it will probably come in a recyclable bottle or can, but do you actually recycle them? Many people don't. If they received money for recycling them, would people recycle more? Statistics from Norway suggest they would. People there get money back when they recycle their plastic drink bottles, which means that nearly 100% of all recyclable drinks bottles in Norway are recycled. If you compare this to other countries, you will see a big difference. Many countries recycle less than 30% of their plastic drink bottles. The Norway model suggests that if these countries introduced similar money-back systems for plastic bottles, global recycling statistics would improve dramatically.

Check!

1 **Read the text above and underline all the conditional sentences.**

Notice

2 **Write an example from the text for conditional sentences with the following patterns.**

a (*if* + present tense) + (*will* + verb)

....

b (*if* + past tense) + (*would* + verb)

....

3 **Match the patterns from Exercise 2 with the correct function below.**

a We use the first conditional to talk about real possibilities that can happen now or in the future. ....

b We use the second conditional to talk about unreal situations that cannot happen or are extremely unlikely to happen now or in the future.

....

4 Find two conditional sentences in the text that use adverbs. Circle the adverbs, then tick the statement below that is true.

In the main clause of a conditional sentence…

A adverbs are always placed after the verb. ☐

B some adverbs can be placed after the verb. ☐

C adverbs are never placed after the verb. ☐

GET IT RIGHT!

Remember that in a second conditional sentence, *were* is often used instead of *was* in the *if* clause. When *were* is used it sounds a little more formal than when *was* is used.

Example:
If recycling ***were*** *a priority, less plastic would end up in our oceans.*

Focus

5 Complete the *if* clause with the verb in brackets, using the correct conditional structure.

a If my cousin .... (buy) a new car, she will buy an electric one.

b If I .... (have) more money, I would donate some to a non-profit organisation.

c If companies .... (reduce) the amount of packaging they use, plastic pollution would also reduce.

d If we .... (not recycle), landfills will fill up faster and new landfill areas will have to be found.

e If the government .... (give) financial support to the non-profit organisation's project, it will have a better chance of being a success.

Practice

6 Match main clauses a–e with the correct *if* clauses i–v.

a If I were you,

b If she were the prime minister,

c If I were a teacher,

d If the city council were more concerned about the environment,

e If plastic were more expensive,

i I would teach children eco-friendly habits from a young age.

ii less of it would be used and more of it would be recycled.

iii she would meet other world leaders to address climate change.

iv they would place recycling bins in the streets and parks.

v I would recycle that bottle.

Challenge

7 Complete these conditional sentences with your own ideas. Write them in your notebook. Pay attention to whether they are first or second conditional sentences.

- If I had enough money,…
- If plastic pollution isn't taken seriously,…
- If one species dies out,…
- If all our waste was dumped into landfills,…
- If more people signed petitions,…

Use of English: Verb forms

USE OF ENGLISH

I want to congratulate you on your excellent work this term and the huge success of our recycling initiative here in school. We have managed to collect 500 kg of plastic, which we will sell to the plastic collection centre. We considered donating the money to an international non-profit organisation but you, the students, have asked us to plant trees in the school grounds instead. If you would like to take part in the tree planting, you should sign up via the school webpage as soon as possible. Finally, as you have shown such interest in the project, we have decided to continue it indefinitely, so please keep on using the recycling bins. Together we can make a difference!

Check!

1 **Read the message from the head teacher. Underline all the examples where the main verb is followed by a second verb. Then write the main verb in the correct place in the list below.**

verb followed by a *to* infinitive: ....

verbs followed by *-ing* form: ....

verbs followed by the bare infinitive (no *to* or *-ing*): ....

....

Notice

2 **What is the name of the group of verbs that are followed by the bare infinitive?**

....

Write down three more verbs from this group. ....

....

Focus

3 **Tick the sentences that are correct. Correct the sentences that are incorrect.**

a More and more people have decided reducing their carbon footprint and now use public transport or share rides with others when they can. ☐

b Instead of using plastic bottles that we throw away after drinking, we must using reusable water bottles to make less plastic waste. ☐

c Sometimes, we might feel like to give up on our efforts to protect the environment, but we have to keep to going and continue what we're doing. ☐

d Some people might dislike composting at home, but it's a great way to reduce the amount of food we throw away and help the soil. ☐

e We should take responsibility for our actions and understand that small changes in our daily lives can have a big impact on the environment. ☐

Practice

4 Put the words in the correct order to make a sentence.

a to / not / the tap water. / drink / The notice / said

....

b use / students / too much paper. / not / encourages / to / The school

....

c at the local beach. / to / instructed / swim / not / The tour guide / me

....

d can't / recycling. / not / I / imagine

....

e considered / but / not / travelling / was an eco-friendly option. / decided / They / a cycling holiday

....

Challenge

5 Read these scenarios. Then complete the sentences with your own ideas. Include some negative forms.

a You have been asked for some suggestions for how to make your school more environmentally friendly.

I suggest ....

b Your friend wants some tips on how to reduce the amount of plastic waste he creates.

I recommend ....

c Your elderly family member has some habits that are not environmentally friendly.

I would encourage them ....

GET IT RIGHT!

Remember that when the second verb needs to be expressed in the negative form, *not* is placed between the main verb and the second verb.

Examples:

I decided ***not*** *to participate in the project.*

He suggested ***not*** *using single-use plastic.*

Improve your writing: Formal emails

1 **Complete the email. Use words from the box, adding capital letters where needed.**

am writing to	cause for concern	firstly	look forward
Sir or Madam	while I understand	would like	

Dear ....[1],

I am a new member of the sports centre, and I have noticed several problems. I ....[2] draw your attention to these problems and suggest solutions.

......................................[3], I have noticed leaking showers in the changing room. An enormous amount of water is being wasted daily. I ....[4] to suggest that you deal with this as an urgent priority. Water is a vital resource that we must all use responsibly.

The second ....[5] is the lighting. I have seen that there are lights on in the building long after the sports centre has closed. ....[6] some security lighting may be necessary, the number of lights left on seems excessive. If smart lighting technology were installed, it would help to tackle this issue.

Looking after the environment is a commitment everyone needs to make. By adopting a more environmentally friendly approach, the image of the sports centre will improve and as a result, membership could even increase.

I hope you have found my suggestions helpful, and I ....[7] to being part of a more responsible sports centre in the near future.

Yours faithfully,

Omar Ogundipe

2 **Read the email again. The email includes all of the following features. Write an example of each.**

a introduce the writer

....

b clearly state the reason for writing

....

c make polite suggestions rather than demand change

....

d acknowledge the reader's perspective

....

e motivate the reader to follow the suggestions

....

f finish with a desire for the future

....

WRITING TIP

In a formal email, the formal tone should be maintained throughout. To create a formal tone, passive structures can be use.

*If smart lighting technology **were installed**, it would help to tackle this issue.*

A formal email can draw on personal experiences and opinions. However, they should be concise and to the point.

I have noticed leaking showers in the male changing room.

3 **Read these tips for writing emails.**
Put a cross next to the tips that do not apply to a formal email.

a Arrange the information in paragraphs. ☐

b Proofread your email before you send it. ☐

c Show you are angry if you are angry; it will make the reader more likely to follow your suggestions. ☐

d Use abbreviated language like *didn't* and *won't*, so it sounds more like spoken English. ☐

e Use the person's name if you know it. If you don't know it, try to find it on a company website. ☐

f Don't write in capital letters; it is the equivalent of shouting at the reader. ☐

4 **Read the task. Use the graphic organiser to help you make notes in your notebook. Then use the notes to write the email.**

Write a formal email to a popular shopping centre, cinema, library or leisure facility in your area. Make suggestions about how its services could be improved.

your relationship to the place (customer, user, visitor, local resident)

....

reason for writing

....

problem that needs improving

....

solution to problem

....

acknowledge reader's perspective

....

how will the reader benefit

....

your desire for the future

....

Check your progress

Vocabulary

1 **Complete the text. Use words from the box.**

environmentally friendly initiatives non-profit organisations petitions single-use plastic

Plastic pollution is one of the major environmental problems of the 21st century, threatening our planet and its wildlife. While people are taking personal action, change is not happening fast enough and more large companies need to address this problem. Signing ....[1] is one way of putting pressure on them. ....[2] also play a vital role in pushing for solutions and raising awareness through their campaigns and conservation ....[3]. Customers need to demand that companies reduce the use of ....[4] and offer us more ....[5] options.

Grammar

2 **Circle the correct word in the sentences below.**

a If you pretend for a moment that we *live* / *lived* without plastic bags, tell me what we would use instead.

b If everyone *agrees* / *agreed*, we will have a picnic and simply spend some time outside in the countryside rather than going to a restaurant in the city.

c If people received money back on all the items they recycled, people *will* / *would* take recycling more seriously.

d So many people refuse *to use* / *using* disposable plastic bags that more and more shops have changed over to paper ones instead.

e An easy way to avoid *to waste* / *wasting* water is to turn off the tap when you are brushing your teeth.

Reading

3 **To what extent are you aware of the impact of your clothes on the environment? Read the text. Does it provide you with any information you were previously unaware of?**

Fast fashion has been identified as a major issue within the fashion industry because of the colossal impact it has on the environment. Fast fashion is defined as clothes that are produced quickly and cheaply, on a huge scale, so that people can buy clothes more often. As a result of the mass production of fashion items, the fashion industry is responsible for more carbon pollution than the air travel and shipping industries combined, and is the second largest consumer of water.

Fortunately, we can fight against the harmful effects of fast fashion. One way is to support fashion brands that have responsible production practices and use eco-friendly materials. Brands that make long-lasting clothing reduce our need to buy new clothes so frequently. Furthermore, as consumers, we need to ask ourselves what we really need before we buy. People currently buy 60% more clothes that they did about 10 years ago but keep their clothes for half the amount of time. However, if we used our clothes for just nine months longer than we currently do, we could reduce their environmental impact by 20–30%. Taking care of our clothes by following proper washing instructions and repairing them can also make them last longer.

Education and awareness play a crucial role in the battle against fast fashion too. Many people are unaware of the extent of its negative impact. Encouraging friends and family to adopt more eco-friendly fashion habits is just as important as reflecting on our own clothing choices. By being more aware of our impact, we can help to transform the fashion industry into one that cares about the environment and supports a better future.

4 **Read the text again.**
Summarise the main points from each paragraph.

Paragraph 1: ....

....

....

....

Paragraph 2: ....

....

....

....

Paragraph 3: ....

....

....

....

Writing

5 **Write a formal email to your school, sports club or a local business that you use frequently and suggest the use of more environmentally friendly uniforms or sports kits for students, members or staff. Write the email in your notebook.**

REFLECTION

Write answers to these questions in your notebook.

a What information did you find most encouraging in this unit?

b What information did you find most worrying?

c Has this unit given you any new ideas about how you can help the environment?

d What issue from this unit do you feel you need to study more?

e What advice would you give to someone making a suggestion in a formal email?

8 Old and new

Think about it: Bridging the generation gap

1 **Read the text. Then answer the questions.**

When I was young my granddad seemed ancient. One of the main reasons for that was that he wasn't physically active any longer and spent most of the day sitting in his favourite armchair. However, he was a fantastic storyteller. He was an experienced traveller too, so he had many tales to tell about faraway places. I would spend hours listening to him. It was a magical time for me and my company was a great comfort to him in his old age.

Even though he was old and couldn't travel any more, he was still very mentally active and interested in the world around him. We didn't experience any of the generation gap you often read about in textbooks. There was a deep sense of trust and understanding between us, and I was able to express my opinions freely. As I spent so much time with him, I was quite mature for my age and my grandfather never looked at my opinions as childish. As I grew older, we would have long and interesting conversations about all kinds of things. I became particularly interested in the stories he told me about his family. My relatives had lived through many changes in my country, so I found my family history fascinating. Thanks to his stories and his encouragement, I actually went on to university to study history. But more importantly, thanks to the relationship I had with him I learnt a valuable life lesson: age is not a barrier to closeness, attitude is.

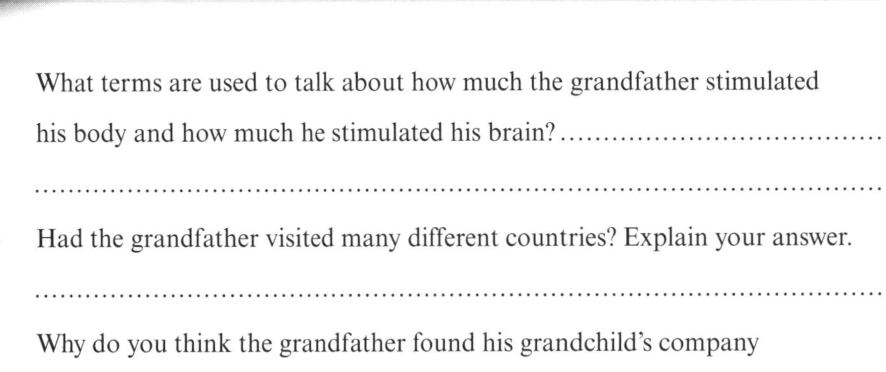

a What terms are used to talk about how much the grandfather stimulated his body and how much he stimulated his brain? ....

....

b Had the grandfather visited many different countries? Explain your answer.

....

c Why do you think the grandfather found his grandchild's company a comfort? ....

d Which word tells us that the writer's grandfather thought it was a good idea that the writer studied history? ....

e Find two different words in the text that are the opposite to mature.

....

f What term does the writer use to explain a lack of understanding that can occur between people of different ages? ....

g How can we tell there was a great sense of trust between them?

....

h Explain in your own words the life lesson that the writer learnt.

....

2 **Match the family anecdotes (a short, often funny, story about real events or people) with one of the words from the box.**

encouragement	good manners	quality time	role models	rules

a I really look up to my aunt and uncle: they always have wise words and look out for others. I hope I can be like them when I'm older. ....

b Balls aren't allowed in my house. My mum got really mad because my sister and I broke her favourite vase one time, so now there is a special box outside where we have to leave them! ....

c What I value most is spending time with my grandparents at their home. I love it there and I always manage to have fun. I'll always remember those moments. ....

d My brothers thought it was great that I studied at art school. They always asked what I was working on and they came to all my exhibitions. I don't think I could have finished it without them. ....

e When I was little I opened my great aunt's fridge to get myself a drink; she was quick to tell me that it wasn't polite to help yourself to food and drinks in other people's houses. I didn't ever do that again! ....

Challenge

3 **In your notebook, write an anecdote from your family based on one of the words from the box in Exercise 2.**

History and technology: How technology is helping ancient archaeology

1 **What problems do you think using technology can cause for archaeologists? Read the article. Does it mention any of the problems you thought of?**

Neal Spencer likes to travel light. Spencer is an archaeologist and keeper of a museum: when he goes on archaeological expeditions, he usually packs notebooks, cameras, laptops, and mosquito nets. Oh, and a lightweight camera drone! 'These days, it's hard to imagine life without it' he told me when we spoke recently. 'And things are so much better when you can fit everything in your **hand baggage**.'

Previously, archaeological excavations operated on a much bigger scale. When German archaeologist Heinrich Schliemann excavated the ancient city of Troy, in what is now northern Turkey, in the 1870s, he employed teams of up to 160 labourers working over three years. These digs were destructive too. Schliemann used dynamite, and scholars later accused him of causing even more damage than the 12th-century BCE Greek invasion.

In contrast, when a **Mayan** megalopolis was uncovered in northern Guatemala in February 2018, archaeologists used a low-flying aircraft equipped with a special camera that allowed researchers to see through the dense jungle **canopy**. They located some 61,000 ancient structures hidden deep beneath the soil, then plotted them onto a virtual 3D environment. No digging necessary – and definitely no dynamite.

Drones have been the true game changer. Instead of organising large-scale expeditions and manually plotting sites inch by inch, Spencer and his colleagues can now send up a flying camera and create a 3D digital model on their laptops in a matter of hours.

Ironically, Spencer pointed out, the danger for archaeologists may now be too much data. The major issue used to be lack of information. Now archaeology is drowning in information: 'Not seeing the wood for the trees, that's the next big problem,' Spencer said.

hand baggage: small cases and bags passengers can take onto a plane

Mayan: ancient indigenous culture from present-day Mexico and Central America

canopy: the leaves and branches of trees that form a kind of roof

ironically: strangely, in a funny way

2 **Read the text again. Match the highlighted words with the definitions below.**

a ....: people who study one subject in great detail, especially at university

b ....: the act of drawing something on a paper in order to make a map

c ....: an extremely large urban area

d ....: a person who is in charge of or takes care of valuable objects

e ....: a product, person or event that completely changes a situation

f ....: projects to dig out old buried objects in order to learn about the past

g ....: a material used to explode the ground

3 **Choose the correct definition for the idiom 'not seeing the wood for the trees', used in the final paragraph of the text.**

A for two people to have a different understanding of the same situation ☐

B to be unable to get an overall understanding of a situation because you are focused on the details ☐

C to try to resolve a problem when you incorrectly believe something is true ☐

Challenge

4 **In your notebook, write a list of the kind of structures that might be discovered at an archaeological site, for example houses, wells, etc.**

....

....

....

....

....

....

Use of English: The third conditional

USE OF ENGLISH

Have you ever thought about the history of your city? What would it have been like if you had lived in your hometown, say, 200 years ago? Museums and guided tours might be a good way to find out even though you're not a tourist. A guide, for example, is trained to explain the history of the town. They would be able to explain how the streets would have looked if you had walked them in the past. They would also certainly tell you that life would not have been easy, especially if you had had to live in the poor neighbourhoods. Cities and the life we lead in them have changed so dramatically over the centuries that sometimes it's hard to understand their complex history. So, should you wish to learn more about your hometown, you might want to consider disguising yourself as a tourist and joining a guided tour!

Check!

1 **Read the text and underline all the sentences with the word *if*. Then read the questions below and tick the correct answer.**

a What kind of sentences are they?

- A First conditional ☐
- B Second conditional ☐
- C Third conditional ☐

b What do the sentences refer to?

- A a past situation that is now impossible ☐
- B a realistic possibility ☐
- C neither of the above ☐

Notice

2 **Look at the verb pattern in the sentences underlined in Exercise 1. Tick the correct pattern below. Remember that the order of the *if* clause and the main clause can change.**

- A (*if* + present simple) + (present simple)
- B (*if* + present simple) + (*will* + verb)
- C (*if* + past simple) + (*would* + verb)
- D (*if* + past perfect) + (*would* + *have* + past participle)

3 **Write an explanation of the third conditional using your answers from Exercises 1 and 2.**

....

....

Focus

4 Rewrite the following sentences in the third conditional.

a I didn't go on the guided tour so I didn't learn about the city.

....

b My parents moved when I was little, so I didn't grow up in my country.

....

c I became fluent in the local language because my grandmother spoke it to me.

....

d Previous generations cut the trees down because they did not understand the impact of their actions.

....

GET IT RIGHT!

Remember neither *would* nor the present perfect are used in the *if* clause.

Example:
The museum visit would have been better if we had had more time. (not *would have had*)

Practice

5 Use the words to write sentences in the third conditional. Remember to use a comma between the clauses in sentences that start with an *if* clause.

a I / cry / if / lose / my grandma's ring.

....

b If / their budget / be / bigger / the city / save / more artefacts.

....

c The indigenous language / not / die out / if / teachers / teach / in schools.

....

d If / better records/ keep/ we/ find out/ more about our ancestors.

....

e If / I / know / it was vintage / I / not throw / it out.

....

Challenge

6 Think of five ways your life would have been different if you had lived 200 years ago. Write your answers in the third conditional.

....

....

....

....

....

Use of English: Present perfect simple and present perfect continuous

USE OF ENGLISH

It seems strange that record stores still exist when most people listen to music on their devices these days. However, the popularity of records, or vinyl as they are also known, **has been increasing** steadily and is likely to continue. While it is true CDs and cassettes **have not had** the same luck, vinyl records **have become** collectors' items. As a result, a lot of record labels **have been releasing** new albums on vinyl lately. Second-hand vinyl records are particularly interesting because, with time, they develop a unique sound. This means the sale of second-hand records **has reached** a new high. For the last decade or so, rare and first edition vinyl records **have been selling** at unbelievable prices. So you may want to ask your granny how many records she **has saved** and whether she wants you to take them down to your local record store!

Check!

1 Read the text. Then tick the tenses that have been used for the verbs in bold.

A present simple ☐
B past continuous ☐
C present perfect simple ☐
D past perfect simple ☐
E past continuous ☐
F present perfect continuous ☐

Notice

2 Use the answers for Exercise 1 to complete these grammar rules.

a We use the ....
- to talk about actions that were completed recently
- to talk about how many or how much
- to emphasise the action.

b We use the ....
- to talk about events that started in the past and are still ongoing
- to emphasise the length of time that has passed.

Focus

3 Correct the mistakes in these sentences. One sentence is correct.

a He's been calling you five times today, he must have something to tell you.

b People have been forgetting the old traditions; they didn't think they were important.

c I've looked for those old photo albums all day and I can't find them anywhere.

d The old market has been knocked down and new apartment blocks have been built instead.

e I've read about the ancient Mayan culture lately; I think it's fascinating.

GET IT RIGHT!

Remember that the present perfect is used with time expressions for a period of time that continues up to the present.

The past simple is used with time expressions for a period of time that has finished.

Examples:
I saw him ***one year ago.***

I haven't seen him ***for a year****.*

I met my cousin for the first time ***last month****.*
(not *have met*)

Practice

4 Circle the correct verb form.

a The new exhibition *has opened* / *opened* yesterday.

b This building *was* / *has been* here for over 200 years.

c The band *released* / *has released* their new album a month ago.

d They *have been building* / *built* that house for ages – will they ever finish it?

e I *have lived* / *lived* here all my life and have no plans of leaving.

Challenge

5 Complete the sentences with the present perfect simple or present perfect continuous. Some sentences can be written with either form. What is the difference in meaning?

a For years I .... (research) my family's past but there are still so many unanswered questions.

b Our family .... (have) this farm for many generations now.

c My father .... (collect) vintage cameras for over 30 years.

d The museum .... (look after) the artefacts so well that they look almost new.

Improve your writing: Informal emails

1 **Read the phrases below. Tick one phrase in each pair suitable for an informal email.**

a i Believe it or not ☐

ii It may be difficult to accept this as true but ☐

b i I am convinced you will be delighted with the event. ☐

ii I think you'll really enjoy it. ☐

c i I would like to inform you ☐

ii I just wanted to let you know ☐

d i Why don't you come…? ☐

ii Would you like to attend…? ☐

WRITING TIP

Remember that emails to friends and family are normally informal. Formal language may sound unfriendly.

Examples:

Do you want to come over for a barbeque? (informal)

You are invited to a barbeque at my house. (formal)

2 **Read the email below. Complete it using suitable phrases from Exercise 1.**

From: tom@email.com

To: darius@email.com

Hi Darius,

Sorry I haven't been in touch for a while. ....[1] about this festival I'm going to be playing at. The band finally got a gig! You see, I **ran into** Mike from school at a party and told him about our group. It **turns out** he studied something to do with the music business and he offered to promote us for free. ....[2], he actually found us a spot at this really cool festival!

It's the Indieshout Festival – have you heard of it? ....[3]. We're going to be playing stuff from our new album to try to **put the word out** about it, but we'll play some old songs too. ....[4] and **check it out**? Lily's group is also playing, so you won't get bored! Do you fancy it?

It's really not good that we haven't seen each other for ages so hope to see you there,

Tom

3 Read the email again. What were Tom's main reasons for writing the email? Circle two options.

- A to complain about something
- B to apologise for something
- C to give some good news
- D to request something
- E to invite someone to something
- F to make an arrangement

4 Read the email again. The underlined words are homonyms, which are words that sound the same but have different meanings. Tick the meaning they have in the email.

a spot

- A to notice something (neutral) ☐
- B a small red mark on someone's skin, especially face, which disappears after time (neutral) ☐
- C a short amount of time in a show given to a performer (neutral) ☐

b stuff

- A possessions (informal) ☐
- B used to refer in a general way to the things that are done or said (informal) ☐
- C to completely fill something with another material (neutral) ☐

c fancy

- A to want to have or do something (informal) ☐
- B decorative (neutral) ☐
- C expensive (informal) ☐

5 Look at the multi-word verbs and idioms in bold in the email. Write their meanings in your notebook. Use a reliable online dictionary to look up the meanings of any verbs or idioms that you do not know.

Challenge

6 Write an informal email to a friend. Tell them about a new event and invite them to go to it with you. Write the email in your notebook.

LANGUAGE TIP

Remember that phrasal verbs and idioms are often informal. A reliable dictionary will usually indicate whether they have a formal or informal meaning.

Examples:

*She **turned up** at my house without calling first.* (informal)

Her arrival was unexpected. (formal)

Check your progress

Vocabulary

1 **Complete the sentences. Use a word or phrase from the box.**

family history	good manners	life lessons
mature	physically active	trust

a To teach me ...., my mum would always tell me to act as if I was having tea with the Queen.

b Asking my granddad about our ...., I found out I have a lot more cousins than I thought!

c If you work on having good exercise habits now, it will be easier to keep .... once you get older.

d We hadn't seen him in years. When he came back he seemed so ...., not the little boy he was when he left!

e The most valuable .... are learnt from your older family members.

f I really .... my older sister; she gives great advice and has always helped me out.

Grammar

2 **Correct the mistakes in these sentences.**

a Have you been losing your great grandmother's ring?

b They have been looking for more artefacts in that archaeological site but have not find any recently.

c My mum has keept all her best clothes to pass on to me; they are vintage now and back in fashion.

d Annie had told stories about her life in the olden days all night – doesn't she ever get tired?

e Local people have been used this ancient path for hundreds of years to move their animals.

Reading

3 **Read the text. Then read the statements. Write True, False or Not given.**

We've all seen vintage cars in films that are set in the late 19th and early 20th centuries, but it's not just filmmakers who like old cars. Collectors pay huge amounts of money for old cars that end up being parked in their garage most of the time. They look good in films but they are definitely not suitable for modern purposes or modern roads.

It may seem strange that people are spending more money on cars which are slower, less comfortable and more wasteful than on modern cars, but this is often the case. These cars would not have space for the average family's weekly grocery shopping, nor do they have the safety features for transporting younger passengers. So they are certainly not a very useful purchase. For this reason, in the vintage car market, specialist mechanics exist who work on the old cars and make sure they meet the minimum standards required for today's needs and today's roads. That said, I'm not sure you'll see many vintage cars parked outside the local shop while their owner runs in to buy some milk; that only happens in the movies!

a Vintage car owners and filmmakers share something in common. ....

b Vintage cars tend to be used on a regular basis. ....

c In their original state, vintage cars do not meet the safety regulations for transporting children. ....

d Certain features of vintage cars are often changed to make them safer. ....

e Vintage car owners love to act out scenes from films. ....

Writing

4 Read the sentences. Are they all formal or informal?

....

We can **hang out** and chill for a bit beforehand.

Why don't you **drop me a line** when you have a sec?

Do you want to **swing by** my place first and **drop off** your stuff?

Let's **dine out** in a fancy restaurant to celebrate – I'll pay!

5 Match the definitions with the phrasal verbs and idioms in bold in Exercise 4.

a ....: to eat an evening meal in a restaurant

b ....: to spend leisure time in a place or with a person

c ....: to visit a place quickly, especially on your way to another place

d ....: to take someone or something to a place and leave them or it there

e ....: to write to someone

6 Write an email to a friend about how the festival mentioned in the Improve your writing lesson went. Invite your friend to another concert. Use the sentences from Exercise 4, if appropriate. Write the email in your notebook.

REFLECTION

Write answers to these questions in your notebook.

a How much do you know about your family history? What else would you like to know?

b How important do you think it is to save artefacts from the past?

c What is the most interesting event in the history of the area that you live in?

d Are vintage items popular in your culture? Why or why not?

e How are informal emails different from formal? Which do you need more practice writing?

9 Tales and stories

Think about it: The joy of reading

1 **Complete the definitions with the correct word or phrase from the box.**

audio book   autobiography   based on a true story comic strip   dialogue   fiction   folk tale   main character moral   narrator   novel   plot   setting   suspense

a ....: an oral story that is passed down from generation to generation.

b ....: a long, made-up story that has been printed into a book.

c ....: an invented story that is inspired by real events.

d ....: the time and place where a story takes place.

e ....: a book that tells the story of a person's life, written by that person.

f ....: a conversation between two or more characters in a story.

g ....: a written story with imaginary people and events rather than a true story.

h ....: the sequence of events in a story.

i ....: a series of drawings that tell a story.

j ....: a type of literature intended to create a feeling of excitement or anxiety that comes from not knowing what is going to happen next.

k ....: a book that has been recorded and is available to listen to.

l ....: a lesson that can be learned from a story.

m ....: the central figure in a story.

n ....: the person who tells the story.

2 Circle the correct word to complete these sentences.

a A young girl who is nervous about starting school is not your typical *moral* / *main character* in an adult novel, but it worked beautifully in this book.

b People often say that the appeal of *fiction* / *autobiography* is the possibility to forget about your problems for a while and explore the imaginative world of the characters.

c I recently read a fascinating novel; the *plot* / *setting* was 18th-century Japan at the time when Mount Fuji erupted.

d The *moral* / *setting* of the story teaches us that even the most unlikely of people can be willing to help and that it is important to never give up hope.

e It's a *comic strip* / *folk tale* that has never been written down but it had been passed down through the generations for centuries.

Challenge

3 Write about your favourite book. Include information about the type of book it is, the main character, the setting and the plot. What type of reader would you recommend it to? Why?

....

....

....

....

....

....

....

Psychology: Why reading books is good for you

It's easy to get sucked into short and **sensational** content on social media. But if you're worried this may be harming your attention span, you should be. There's solid evidence that so many demands on our attention make us more stressed and that the endless social comparison makes us feel worse about ourselves.

For better mental health, read a book. Studies show a range of psychological benefits from reading books. Reading fiction can increase your **capacity** for empathy, through the process of seeing the world through a **relatable** character. Reading has been found to reduce stress as effectively as yoga. It is being prescribed for depression, a treatment known as bibliotherapy.

Tips to get back into books

If you are having difficulty choosing between your phone and a book, here is one simple tip proven by behavioural science. To change behaviour, it also helps to change your environment.

So try the following:

- Carry a book in your bag at all times, or leave books around the house in convenient places.
- Schedule reading time into your day. Twenty minutes is enough. This **reinforces** the habit and ensures regular immersion in the book world.
- If you're not enjoying a book, try another. Don't force yourself.

sensational: shocking or exciting rather than factual

capacity: a person's ability to do a certain activity

relatable: easy to understand

reinforce: to support, make stronger

1 **Read the article on the previous page. Then draw a line from each psychological term to the correct meaning.**

attention span	a	anything that promotes healthier thoughts and mental processes
behavioural science	b	the act of becoming completely involved in one activity and shutting out others
empathy	c	the study of how humans behave
immersion	d	the ability to imagine what it would be like to be in another person's situation
psychological benefits	e	the amount of time someone can concentrate on a task or activity

2 **Reread the article. Then read the statements. Write True, False or Not given.**

a The positive feeling of finishing a book trains readers to complete things they have set out to do. ....

b It is better to put your book in your bag than leave it on the table if you want to improve your reading habits. ....

c Extreme social media use affects our stress levels and the amount of time we can concentrate. ....

d The advantages of reading on our physical and mental health have been proven. ....

e If you want to become a better reader, it's better to keep changing books until you find one you like. ....

f Feeling empathy for a fictional character in a difficult situation can add to your stress levels. ....

g Books cannot reduce anxiety in the way yoga does. ....

h Doctors may recommend reading if you are feeling down. ....

Challenge

3 **Think of three more tips for improving your reading habits.**

....

....

....

Use of English: Direct speech

USE OF ENGLISH

'Come in!' she said in a kind voice and smiled.

Sunshine shone through the window, making the room look bright and cheery. She indicated with her hand that I should sit down.

'Thank you!' I said, starting to feel a little calmer. She poured two glasses of water, then handed me one of them.

'How can I help you, Dastan?' she asked. 'I understand you have a question.'

I felt my hands start to sweat again.

'Yes, I do. I wanted to ask you,' I said in a quiet voice, 'if you could teach me to ride a bike.'

'A bike? Ride a bike? Yes, of course I can! When shall we start?'

Check!

1 **Read the extract from a novel above.**
Underline the words that the characters in the story say.

Notice

2 **Read the extract again and answer these questions.**

a What punctuation marks are used to separate the words the characters say from the rest of the story? ....

b Are the sentences and phrases inside the speech marks punctuated? ....

c Is the first letter inside the speech mark always a capital letter? If not, explain why not.

....

d Where in the sentence can the reporting clause (the clause that tells the reader who is speaking) be placed? Is it always placed after the direct speech?

....

e When a new person speaks, is what they say placed on the same line as the last speaker or on a new line? ....

3 **Read the final line of the dialogue again.**
Then answer the questions with a Yes or a No. Finally, complete the rule.

a Is there a reporting clause? ....

b Is it clear who is speaking? ....

c Does the context make it clear who is speaking? ....

d It is not necessary to use a reporting clause when ....

Focus

4 Rewrite the following dialogue with the correct punctuation.

Sam and Asha ran into the house. Hi Mum, we're home they shouted at the same time. I'm in the kitchen, come on through. She kissed them and told them to wash their hands and sit down. It was amazing, Mum said Asha. Yeah, it was brilliant added Sam. Well, here eat these she said sitting down at the table with a plate of sandwiches and tell me all about it.

....

....

....

....

....

....

Practice

5 Copy these reporting verbs into your notebook and add as many other reporting verbs as you can think of.

shout | sing | whisper

6 Rewrite the dialogue below using the tips in the Get it Right box. Complete the text with your own ideas.

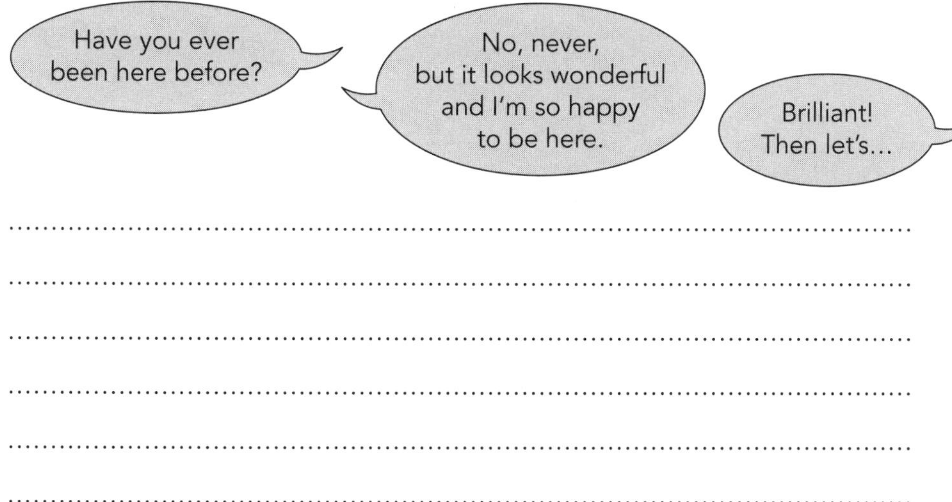

....

....

....

....

....

....

Challenge

7 Think of a conversation you had earlier today. Write it in your notebook as a dialogue.

GET IT RIGHT!

Remember, varying the position of the reported clause in the sentence and the reporting verb you use can help to make the story more interesting.

Examples:

He refused, *'No, I'm not going to do that.'*

*'No,' **he complained**, 'I'm not going to do that.'*

*'No, I'm not going to do that,' **he protested**.*

Use of English: Narrative verb forms – past simple, past perfect and past continuous

USE OF ENGLISH

We **woke up** cold and wet inside the shelter we **had made** the night before. It was still early and the air felt damp. The fire **had gone out**. We **crawled** out of the shelter and **gathered** whatever dry branches we **found**. The fire we **lit** was small but it **warmed** our hands. I **went** down to the stream and **collected** some water. When I returned, Valentina was preparing the breakfast. We didn't have much food left. I **had never eaten** a peanut butter and tomato sandwich before but it tasted good. We were finishing our tea when I heard a noise. There was a bear on the other side of the fire. I **wondered** what he was thinking.

Check!

1 **Read the story. Were the following verb forms used? Circle the correct answer, Yes or No.**

a	present simple	Yes	No
b	present continuous	Yes	No
c	past simple	Yes	No
d	past continuous	Yes	No
e	past perfect simple	Yes	No
f	past perfect continuous	Yes	No
g	Are all the events described in the order that they happened (chronological order)?	Yes	No

Notice

2 **Look at the verbs in bold in the story and circle the correct tense to complete the grammar rules.**

a We use the .... to describe the events of a story in chronological order.
   A past simple   B past continuous   C past perfect simple

b We use the .... to describe the events of a story that are not in chronological order.
   A past simple   B past continuous   C past perfect simple

3 **Look at the underlined verbs in the story. Then answer the questions and circle the correct word in the grammar rule.**

a Do they describe an action? ....

b Do they describe a state without an action? ....

c Are they written in the past simple or past continuous? ....

d We use the *past simple / past continuous* to describe a state without an action.

CONTINUED

4 Look at the highlighted sentences in the story, which contain two action verbs. Tick the sentence(s) below that are true.

A We use the past simple form to describe an action in progress in the past and past continuous for a shorter action that interrupted it. ☐

B We use the past continuous form to describe an action in progress in the past and past simple for a shorter action that interrupted it. ☐

Focus

5 Correct these sentences.

a Rebecca was never eating Polish food.

b He noticed that snow had block the road.

c While she was walking home, the street lights were going black.

Practice

6 Write the verbs in brackets in the correct form.

a As I walked through the park, the wind .... (blow) so hard that a huge branch suddenly .... (bend) and .... (break) right in front of me.

b I had to wait until late at night to open my present, as my mother .... (forbid) me to open it without her.

c We .... (know) each other for years but we .... (not recognise) each other straight away.

d The students .... (complain) about the classrooms for years but no one .... (ever take) their complaints seriously.

GET IT RIGHT!

Remember that many verbs are irregular in the past simple and past perfect. For some irregular verbs, the past simple and past participle are different.

Examples:

*The children **took** out their map but they didn't know where they were.* (past simple)

*They **had taken** the wrong path and couldn't find the way home.* (past perfect)

Challenge

7 Describe a trip you made in the past. Try to use examples of all the past verb forms. To be able to include examples of the past perfect, you can mention the preparations you had made before leaving. Write the paragraph in your notebook.

Improve your writing: A short story

1 Use the graphic organisers to organise the ideas for Story 1 and Story 2.

Story 1

- curious child with habit of wandering off on own
- child finds grandmother after accident in forest and brings her home
- small village in Africa
- child lost and alone in forest
- wise, old lady with lots of patience
- a grandmother teaches her grandchild a life lesson
- grandmother takes child to forest many times, each time showing landmarks and letting child wander a little further on own

Plot:	....
Setting:	....
Storyline:	**Beginning:** ....
	Middle: ....
	Ending: ....
Main character/s:	....

Story 2

- one day, while playing football, they notice an old man has left his wallet on park bench, but they have to find out who he is to be able to return it
- two playful, adventurous brothers
- two brothers find a way to return a lost wallet
- two brothers play football in city park every day, often coincide with the same people in park
- brothers find out who old man is and return wallet to him
- old man who is well-known in neighbourhood
- inner-city neighbourhood

Plot:	....
Setting:	....
Storyline:	**Beginning:** ....
	Middle: ....
	Ending: ....
Main character/s:	....

2 **Read the writing tasks.**
Match the two story outlines in Exercise 1 with the writing tasks.

a

Win the short story competition!

Write a story for the school short story competition.
Your story must **begin** with the sentence:

It was cold outside but they didn't mind.

Your story must include:

- a lost object
- a well-known person.

b

We need stories for the new school blog!

Write a short story for the school blog.
Your story must **begin** with the sentence:

She noticed a path she had never seen before and decided to see where it went.

Your story must include:

- a kind elderly lady
- a loud noise.

3 **Complete these sentences with the most suitable expression of time or place from the box.**

By early afternoon, Just before I arrived, On the park bench, Outside the cinema, Straight after his exam,

a .... there was a line of people waiting in the rain for the film to start.

b .... I received a strange message saying the plans had changed.

c .... the girl found a note with her name on it.

d .... the park was full of young families playing and eating ice-creams.

e .... he called his mum to say thank you.

WRITING TIP

Expressions of time and place can help the reader to follow the sequence of events in a story.

Examples:
In the school playground, I bumped into my old Spanish teacher and that got me thinking.

By midday, I was exhausted and just wanted to go home.

4 **Choose one of the writing tasks from Exercise 2 and write your own short story. You can use the ideas from Exercise 1 or ideas of your own. Write the story in your notebook.**

Check your progress

Vocabulary

1 **Complete these sentences with words from the box. There are some extra words that are not needed.**

autobiography	comic strips	fiction	
main character	moral	novel	setting

a The .... of the story is a remote mountain village, where the characters have limited access to modern technology.

b The .... I'm reading is written by a famous musician who shares their journey and experiences in the music industry.

c It's simply not true that .... are only suitable for children's stories; they combine humour and visual storytelling in a way that can be entertaining for adults too.

d The book won the prize because the .... of the story is so relevant today; honesty and kindness are the keys to a happier life.

Grammar

2 **Correct the mistakes in the sentences.**

a I payed the bill and went straight home, hoping I would never see him again.

b We were rehearsing for months, but I still didn't feel ready on the opening night.

c When I saw the present I knew immediately that it had costed a lot of money.

d This is where I live he whispered quietly.

e 'Can you help me?' 'I really don't understand and I can't do it on my own.' she asked.

Reading

3 **Read the article. Then answer the questions that follow.**

1 There are many benefits to bedtime stories; however, it's not just limited to creating magical memories and forming part of a routine that will help young children to fall asleep.

2 In fact, bedtime stories are proven to help create a bond between parents and children, lower kids' stress levels and improve their literacy skills and **mastery** of language.

3 'We know now, because we have brain imaging studies, that there's a difference in the reading and **cognitive skills** of kids whose parents sit with them and read. The difference has nothing to do with things like family background, their home environment or **socioeconomic** status, but how frequently an adult sits and reads with the child,' says psychologist Collett Smart, a mother of three who has 20 years of experience as a classroom teacher.

4 'When kids are read to every day there's a significant positive impact on their reading skills and cognitive skills like numeracy. We see benefits in their development right up until about the age of 11, and those benefits last later in life.'

mastery: great knowledge and understanding of a subject

cognitive skills: the mental processes used to think, learn, remember, reason, etc.

socioeconomic: related to a combination of social and economic factors

Which paragraph (1–4) mentions the following?

a the importance of a daily story time routine ☐

b positive moments that will be remembered ☐

c a reduction in childhood anxiety ☐

d non-academic factors that were also studied ☐

e a strong emotional connection ☐

f long-term advantages for personal growth ☐

g advanced technology that helps to understand the brain ☐

Writing

4 Read the tips.
Tick which tips are true for writing a story.

A It's best to invent the story as you write it. ☐

B We normally use the past verb forms to write a story. ☐

C Don't describe what the characters can see, hear or smell; it doesn't help the reader. ☐

D Use direct speech to make the story more interesting and realistic. ☐

E Punctuation and paragraphs are not important in stories. ☐

F Use expressions of time and place to help the reader follow the sequence of events. ☐

5 Read the writing task. Copy the graphic organiser into your notebook. Complete the plan with your ideas for your story, then write the story in your notebook.

Stories needed!

Write a story for the school magazine.
Your story must **begin** with the sentence:

When I opened the door I couldn't believe my eyes.

Your story must include:

- a policeman
- a box of chocolates.

Plot:	....	
Setting:	....	
Storyline:	**Beginning:**	....
	Middle:	....
	Ending:	....
Main character/s:	....	
Secondary character:	....	

REFLECTION

Write answers to these questions in your notebook.

a Do you think you read enough? How might you benefit from reading more?

b What type of books do you enjoy most? Explain your answer.

c Give an example, other than for studying, when reading has helped you in some way.

d Is there a book that you would like to read but haven't? Why haven't you?

e What do you find hardest about writing a story? How can you improve this?

10 Looking ahead

Think about it: Choosing a future career

1 **Read the students' comments about what type of working conditions they would like when they start working. Suggest a job from the box that fits the characteristics mentioned in each comment. More than one job may be suitable.**

carpenter	journalist	marketing manager	musician	programmer
technician	translator	vet	visual effects digital artist	

a **Lameh**

I don't mind working for a low salary in the beginning as long as the company can offer long-term prospects that would see me slowly working my way up to a better position, more responsibility and a decent salary.

Job suggestion: ....

b **Omar**

Apprenticeships are a great option. I like them because they are the best way to learn a trade. When it's a job that you do with your hands, it's much more fulfilling to train by doing practical tasks rather than reading a textbook. It suits the way I like to learn.

Job suggestion: ....

c **Ava**

External competition can be inspiring and help to stimulate the workforce to work together, but when it is internal, between co-workers, it has the opposite effect. Either way, I believe it leads to more high-pressured environments and higher stress levels, so I'd rather avoid it. I don't work well in those conditions.

Job suggestion: ....

d **Leeman**

Honestly, I would just like to work doing something that is related to my hobbies: animals and music. I believe job satisfaction is really important, and that it's closely related to how interesting you find your work. When you're doing something you like, your workload feels much lighter.

Job suggestion: ....

e 

Salma

We live in the digital age and I want to take advantage of that. I want the possibility of working from home with flexible working hours. I know that this means you don't have a clear distinction between home life and work, so there's a risk you end up working a lot of overtime, but I'm fairly good at planning my time and switching off the computer when it's time to relax.

Job suggestion: ....

2 **Which student mentions the following?**

a the possibility to choose the times you work ....

b the positive and negative effects of work being like a contest ....

c learning professional skills by working rather than studying ....

d the possibility of eventually being well-paid ....

e the danger of working more hours than you are officially supposed to ....

f the amount of work you have feeling less when you enjoy what you do ....

3 **Find a synonym in the text in Exercise 1 for each of the following words.**

a staff ....

b rewarding ....

c colleagues ....

d demanding ....

Challenge

4 **Read the following job characteristics. Write a short answer in your notebook to say whether you would or would not like to work under these working conditions in your future career.**

- a decent salary but high pressure
- flexible working hours but not fulfilling
- external competition

Human geography and environmental science: 15-minute cities

1 **Imagine what cities will be like by 2050. Write your ideas in your notebook.**

2 **Read the article below. Are any of your ideas from Exercise 1 mentioned?**

Predictions state that by 2050, two out of every three people on the planet will be living in cities and urban environments. The number of megacities – cities with more than 10 million inhabitants – will have increased to nearly 50 globally and many of those will have over 20 million residents. A hundred years ago there were no megacities at all.

Large urban areas mean large urban problems – traffic congestion and pollution, for example. However, the concept of 15-minute cities, which involves cities having many **hubs**, offers a solution. Everything residents need on a daily basis would be available within a 15-minute walking or cycling distance. This would include shops, schools, workplaces, parks and sports facilities. The 15-minute city would reduce dependence on cars and address many of the current urban problems.

Before city dwellers had cars, this was, in fact, how cities were organised. Each neighbourhood had its own centre where most services were available. This changed as residents became car owners, out-of-city shopping malls became popular and commuting long distances to work became the norm. Many of these old neighbourhood centres fell into decline. However, the infrastructure often still exists, making it much easier to recreate these 15-minute living spaces.

Climate change is one of the main factors pushing us back towards this old-fashioned style of urban planning. The need to reduce carbon emissions and to capture more of the emissions that are released is growing in urgency. Furthermore, people living in cities are increasingly looking for a better balance in their urban lifestyles and a greater sense of community. The 15-minute city may well offer a popular solution for healthy urban living in the future.

hub: a central or main area where there is lots of activity

3 **What is the main purpose of the article? Tick the correct answer.**

A to stop the development of megacities ☐

B to promote the idea of self-contained urban neighbourhoods ☐

C to encourage city dwellers not to use their cars ☐

4 **Read the article again. Complete the tasks below.**

a Find three synonyms to describe the people who live somewhere.

....

b Find an expression that means something becomes lesser in importance and quality. ....

c Find a noun that refers to the basic structure (buildings, transport systems, electricity, etc.) needed for an area or organisation to run smoothly.

....

d Find a compound noun that describes the process of designing towns and cities so they are pleasant, well-functioning areas to live in.

....

5 **Answer these questions with short answers.**

a Do you think modern technology would make living in cities organised around hubs better or worse than in the past? Briefly explain why.

....

....

b As 'green' transport becomes more common, do you think we need 15-minute cities? Briefly explain why.

....

....

Challenge

6 **Do you have access to everything you need on a daily basis within 15 minutes on foot or by bike? Imagine living in the opposite situation. What difference would it make to your life or your family's life? Write your ideas in your notebook.**

Use of English: Time adverbials used with the past simple and present perfect

USE OF ENGLISH

This summer I'm going to South America with my friend and I'm so excited! We've been planning it over the last few months to make sure we have the best time possible.

It all started last winter. We researched the countries we want to visit. Afterwards, we planned out our budget. I have been saving up for over a year but I will still need to keep track of my expenses and make sure I don't run out of money.

We have already booked places to stay. I found a bunch of really cool hostels. Last week, we booked our flights. So now we're all set to go. I can't wait! It's going to be something I'll remember forever.

Check!

1 **Read the text. Underline all the words and expressions that refer to a time in the past.**

Notice

2 **Match the beginnings of the explanations with the correct endings.**

We use words like *already* and the present perfect

We use words like *for over a year* and the present perfect continuous

We use words like *afterwards* and the past simple

a to talk about specific moments in the past and finished actions.

b to emphasise that something happened in the past but is connected to the present.

c to emphasise the period of time during which an unfinished action has occurred.

Focus

3 **Circle the correct verb to complete the sentences.**

a I *had / have had* an incredible vacation with my family at the beach last summer. We *have spent / spent* a week playing in the sand and swimming in the ocean.

b I *have been visiting / visited* Paris two years ago. It *has been / was* such an amazing experience to explore the beautiful streets of the city.

c I *have just finished / was just finishing* a pottery course. It *was / was being* so much fun to work with clay.

Practice

4 Correct the mistakes. One sentence is correct.

a The last week I dropped out of the trip – I was exhausted and just wanted to go home.

b Many people with low-paid jobs don't have any money left by last week of the month.

c Changes to the education system were made the year before last but it's only now that the results are noticeable.

d For last few years, interest in apprenticeships has steadily increased.

e As of the last week, the entire workforce is able to choose flexible working hours if they wish.

GET IT RIGHT!

Remember *the* is not used in time adverbials like *last month*. However, *the* is used in time adverbials like *the month before last.*

Examples:
Last month, *I went to Ghana.*

I finished the course ***the month before last.*** (that is, two months ago)

Challenge

5 Complete the text with words from the box.

already	few weeks	for	just	since	six months ago	yet

Predicting what you will want in the future is difficult! ....[1] many years I have been planning on being a chemist. However, ...[2] the new school library opened I have been going there nearly every day and I have realised what I really like is reading. So ....[3], I signed up for a literature course. A ....[4] after starting, I decided to spend the summer in Spain and learn more about its literature. I have ....[5] arrived and I'm amazed by the place, so now my goal is to make a film about the Spanish way of life. I have ....[6] started writing the script but I haven't started filming ....[7]. From chemistry to filmmaking; that's quite a change!

Use of English: Indirect questions

USE OF ENGLISH

Karen: Hello, I'm Karen, from Shrewsbury Secondary School. I called last week to ask about a school trip to the museum. I was wondering if I could ask a few more questions.

Museum receptionist: Ah yes, I remember, thanks for calling again. Yes, of course, how can I help you?

Karen: Well, I would like to know what is included in the basic school trip package.

Museum receptionist: It includes access to the Prehistoric exhibition, all the national history rooms and the Medieval Europe exhibition.

Karen: May I ask if you provide guides who can lead the students through the different rooms?

Museum receptionist: Yes, of course, that's also included! Would you mind telling me how many students you will bring to the museum?

Karen: I can't give an exact number at the moment but approximately 60 students, I think.

Museum receptionist: OK, that's fine. We place one guide for each group of 20. So, would you be able to divide the students into three groups before arriving at the museum?

Check!

1 **Read the conversation. Underline all the expressions used to change questions from direct questions into indirect questions.**

Notice

2 **Read the expressions and the sentences they are in again. Then circle True or False for these statements about indirect questions.**

a	The main clauses use the same word order as questions.	True	False
b	The main clauses do not use the auxiliary verb *do*.	True	False
c	All indirect questions end with a question mark.	True	False
d	*If* or *whether* are used in yes/no questions.	True	False

Focus

3 Correct the mistakes.

a Would you mind telling me what time are you going to arrive?

b Can you tell me what is the best bus to take?

c I would like to ask how do you book the tickets?

d I was wondering, is there a café at the museum?

e May I ask what time does the museum open?

Practice

4 Match the beginnings of the indirect questions with the correct ending (a–c).

Could you tell me if	a	the hotel is near the train station or not?
I was wondering whether	b	the museum is open on Saturdays?
May I ask whether	c	or not I can buy the tickets online.

Challenge

5 Write indirect questions for each of the following situations.

a You would like an extension for a school project.

....

b You need to ask someone on the street where the library is.

....

c You have a seat reserved on a train. Someone is sitting in your seat.

....

d You would like to meet a teacher after class so they can explain something you don't understand.

....

GET IT RIGHT!

Notice that it is correct to use *or not* after *whether*. It is not correct to use *or not* after *if*.

Examples:

*Do you happen to know **whether or not** the guides speak English?*

*Do you happen to know **whether** the guides speak English **or not**?*

*Do you happen to know **if** the guides speak English?*

Improve your writing: A formal email requesting information

1 **Read the email below and the tips for writing a formal letter. Then tick the tips that have been followed and correct the email in the places where the tips have not been followed.**

From: j.faraji@email.com

To: info@fantail.design.com

Dear Sir/Madam,

My name is John Faraji. I'm 17 years old and am currently studying art and design at Sierra Community College. I'm writing to ask about the possibility of doing a work experience placement at your company.

I'm a great admirer of the work your company does, not only for the quality and creativity of the designs but also for your commitment to promoting local businesses. I follow you on social media and I am familiar with the projects that you do.

As part of my course, I'm required to do a work placement for three months. I'd very much like to do this at your company. I'd be grateful if you could tell me whether or not you have work placement students. If you do, would you be able to tell me what the entry requirements are?

I'd be happy to do any project you feel would benefit from my collaboration. I'm particularly interested in the design aspect of my course and I have sound knowledge of various graphic design programs. My teachers are able to give references, should you want them.

I look forward to hearing from you soon.

Thanks,
John

How to write a formal email

- use formal salutations at the beginning and end of the email ☐
- avoid multi-word verbs if better alternatives exist ☐
- don't use abbreviated verb forms ☐
- use indirect questions for requests ☐

2 Read the email again. Then where suitable, change the verbs in the email for a more formal alternative from the box. The form of the verb may need to be changed.

accept collaborate on complete enquire explain inform participate in produce provide require

WRITING TIP

Verbs like *have, do, get, give*, etc. often have formal alternatives that can be used when writing. Which verb is a suitable alternative will depend on the context in which the verb is being used.

Examples:

The company ***has*** *a variety of services.* (informal)

The company ***offers*** *a variety of services.* (formal)

3 Read the writing task. Then use the graphic organiser to plan your email.

You and some other students from your design class are interested in visiting an architect's studio to find out more about their profession. Contact a local architect firm and ask whether you can visit.

Your email should include:

- why you chose that company
- what you would like to see
- a request for a question and answer session.

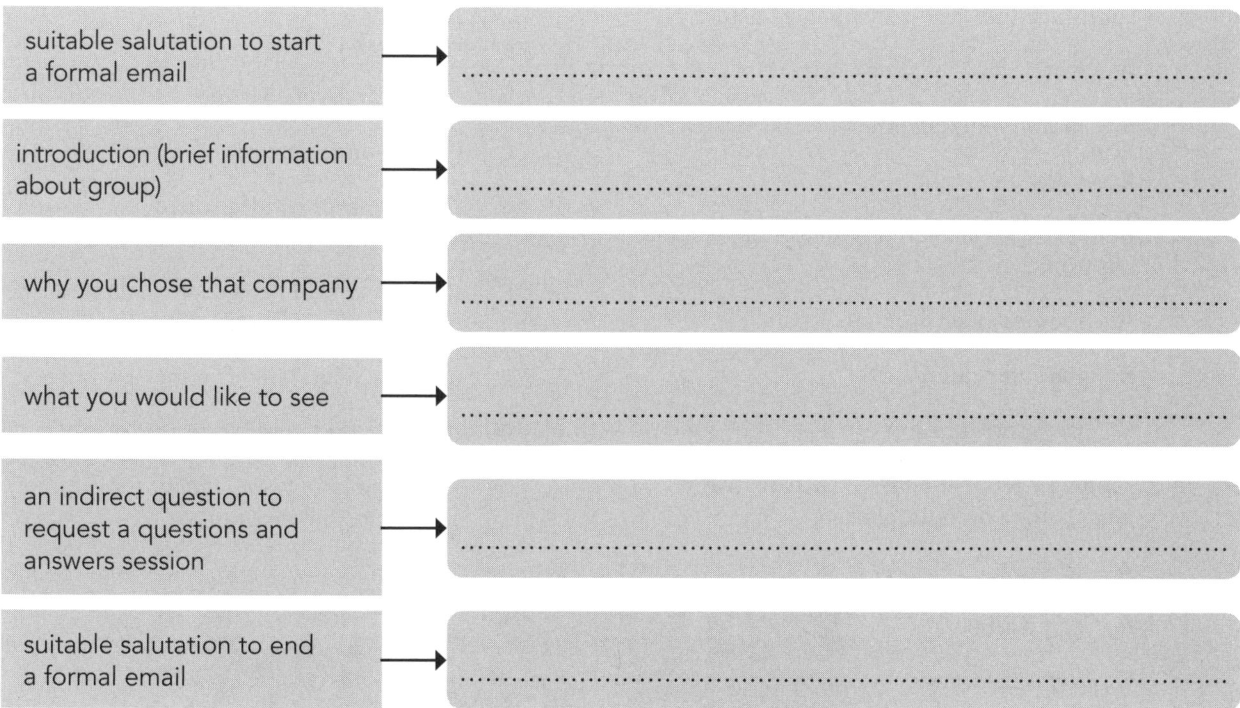

4 Use your notes from Exercise 3, the tips from Exercise 1 and the writing tip to write your email in your notebook. Write 150–200 words.

Check your progress

Vocabulary

1 **Circle the correct word to complete these sentences.**

a Most people accept that first jobs do not give decent ....

A overtime

B workload

C salaries

b Many employees are willing to work .... in order to meet deadlines.

A overtime

B a workload

C an apprenticeship

c Having a decent salary and .... can contribute to a healthy work–life balance.

A workforce

B flexible working hours

C overtime

d In today's job market, it is important to stand out from ....

A the co-workers

B the competition

C the apprenticeship

e Finding a job that offers .... can greatly impact one's overall wellbeing.

A workforce

B competition

C job satisfaction

Grammar

2 **Correct the mistakes in these sentences. One sentence is correct.**

a I haven't been visiting my dream destination yet, but I hope to go there next year.

b At the beginning of November, I had organised a surprise birthday party for my classmate.

c A year ago, I started learning how to play the guitar. It has been fun and I can already play a few songs.

d I already decided what I want to do in the future, so I am doing voluntary work to get some experience.

3 **Match the beginnings (a–d) and endings (i–iv) of the indirect questions.**

a May I ask if

b I was wondering whether

c Could you tell me who

d Do you have any idea where

i the company offers a decent salary for the entry-level positions.

ii my co-workers will be in the new project?

iii it's common to work overtime here?

iv I can find information about the apprenticeship programme?

Reading

4 **Read the article. Who is the intended audience?**

Your first job is often the hardest job to find. Many employers require some sort of experience, even though they are only offering low-skilled or low-paid work. It is common for young people to feel like it is impossible to break into the job market – it can be very challenging.

Voluntary work offers a solution. It can provide that valuable experience which employers are looking for. Furthermore, there is not usually the same kind of competition between volunteers so it can be a smoother introduction to the workplace.

Volunteering is a way of exploring what kind of work you want too. There is no limit: you can try as many volunteer workplaces, tasks and roles as you want. Alternatively, it can help to meet people in the industry if you already have a clear idea of where you want to work.

Even though it is unpaid, all this experience will look good on your CV and fill it out if it looks a bit empty. So what are you waiting for? Go on, try it out. Apart from helping the community you will also be helping yourself!

5 **Which statement best describes the main idea of the text? Tick the correct answer.**

A Employers should make it easier for young people to get their first job. ☐

B Voluntary work is good when you don't know anyone in the field you want to work in. ☐

C Voluntary work can be used as a stepping stone into your first paid work. ☐

Writing

6 **Read the email below. In your notebook, write a list of suggestions of how it could be improved. Include some examples.**

Hi there!

How do I become a volunteer at your organisation? I have been checking out your work and I'm inspired by the positive impact you make in the community.

I'm interested in volunteering because I believe in giving back and making a difference in people's lives. Your organisation's views are the same as mine. I'd love to give my time and skills to help you out.

I've got some questions:

- How many other volunteers there are?
- How old are the other volunteers?
- What days and times do they typically volunteer?

Write back soon,

Cheers,
Priya

REFLECTION

Write answers to these questions in your notebook.

a What is your biggest goal for the future?

b What problems will your local area have to overcome in the near future? What solutions should be considered?

c In your opinion, do we think too much or too little about the future? Support you answer with examples.

d What situations might you find yourself in, in the near future, where you may have to request something in a polite manner?

e Do you find it more difficult to write a formal or informal email in English? Explain your answer.

Key phrases bank

Unit 1

Speculating

I suppose this could be true…
I think it's unlikely that…

Talking about preferences

I prefer…
I enjoy…
I find… really helpful, more than anything else.

Comparing your own experiences with other people's

Just like you, I preferred… for the same reason.
Unlike you, I really enjoyed learning to… because…

Unit 2

When you don't know the answer to a question

Sorry, I have no idea what the answer is.
Sorry, but I don't really know anything about orangutan schools.
I haven't a clue – sorry.

To express surprise

Wow! That's really amazing!
I didn't know that was possible.
This is so incredible, isn't it?

Expressing opinion about which option to choose

I really feel that… would be the best option because…
I'd like to point out that… would probably be the best activity to include, because…

Unit 3

Reacting to what others say

That's a very interesting choice.
Oh really?
Where did you learn all this?
Me too!
I feel a bit differently about this.

Expressing a strong surprise

I can't get over the fact that…
I'm really shocked by…
I'm absolutely speechless.

Unit 4

Adding emphasis

That's absolutely amazing.
It does look stunning.
Yes, they certainly have!

Reacting to what others have said

That's right.
That's a very good question.
You've just made a very good point!
Oh, I love that.

Unit 5

Reporting results and expressing your opinion

Most students thought that…, which I find really surprising.
Some students suggested…, which I think is a very good idea.

Unit 6

Expressing probability and certainty

... the chances are...
... most likely to...
... may well...
... will...

Linking words and phrases

On (the) one hand,...
Although...
Even though...
However,...
Nevertheless...
Despite...
In spite of...
As well as...
In addition to...
Moreover,...
Furthermore, ...
What is more...
Additionally...

Unit 7

Taking turns in discussions

Speaking of...
That's exactly what I was thinking.
Wouldn't you agree?
That's right. And I believe that...
What's it about, exactly?

Unit 8

Greeting and signing off phrases in emails

Hi
Hello
Dear...
Hey there,
Best wishes
All the best
Kind regards
Regards

Unit 9

Making your message more powerful

You would be really helping us out if you could...
We urgently need your help with...

Unit 10

Saying how important something is

I feel it's vital to...
It might be useful to...
I don't think it's absolutely necessary to...

Asking questions or commenting at the end of a presentation

Thank you, that was very interesting, but could you tell us a bit more about...?
I didn't know that..., so it was very interesting to hear about it.

Irregular verb table

Infinitive	Past simple	Past participle
be	was, were	been
begin	began	begun
break	broke	broken
bring	brought	brought
buy	bought	bought
build	built	built
choose	chose	chosen
come	came	come
cost	cost	cost
cut	cut	cut
do	did	done
draw	drew	drawn
drive	drove	driven
eat	ate	eaten
feel	felt	felt
find	found	found
fly	flew	flown
get	got	got
give	gave	given
go	went	gone
have	had	had
hold	held	held
hurt	hurt	hurt
keep	kept	kept
know	knew	known
leave	left	left
lead	led	led
let	let	let
lie	lay	lain
lose	lost	lost
make	made	made
mean	meant	meant
meet	met	met
pay	paid	paid
put	put	put
run	ran	run

Infinitive	Past simple	Past participle
say	said	said
see	saw	seen
sell	sold	sold
send	sent	sent
set	set	set
sit	sat	sat
speak	spoke	spoken
spend	spent	spent
stand	stood	stood
take	took	taken
teach	taught	taught
tell	told	told
think	thought	thought
understand	understood	understood
wear	wore	worn
win	won	won
write	wrote	written

Acknowledgements

The authors and publishers acknowledge the following sources of copyright material and are grateful for the permissions granted. While every effort has been made, it has not always been possible to identify the sources of all the material used, or to trace all copyright holders. If any omissions are brought to our notice, we will be happy to include the appropriate acknowledgements on reprinting.

Unit 7 Text adapted from 'Action for Nature 2022 Eco Hero winners list', used with the permission of Action for Nature; **Unit 8** Text adapted from 'How Cutting-Edge Tech Is Empowering Ancient Archaeology', by Andrew Dickson, 27 June 2019, used with the permission of Andrew Dickson, published by Medium; **Unit 9** Text adapted from 'Why reading books is good for society, wellbeing and your career', by Meg Elkins, Jane Fry and Lisa Farrell, 12 April 2023, used with the permission of The Conversation; Text adapted from 'Why bedtime stories are so important', by Kirrily Schwarz, used with the permission, published by News Life Media.

Thanks to the following for permission to reproduce images:

Cover Weiguan Lin/GI; **Unit 1** FG Trade/GI; Carol Yepes/GI; Westend61/GI; SDI Productions/GI; SimplyCreativePhotography/GI; Mikolette/GI; Kong Ding Chek/GI; Liliboas/GI; SolStock/GI; **Unit 2** Diana Robinson/GI; Reinhard Dirscherl/GI; Paul Souders/GI; Sciepro/GI; Kevin Schafer/GI; Kristian Bell/GI; Life On White/GI; Arun Roisri/GI; Troy Harrison/GI; Adrian Wombwell/500px/GI; Trey Thomas/GI; Mark Newman/GI; Darren Langdon/GI; James Warwick/GI; Jack Davison/GI; Adam Gault/GI; **Unit 3** Kali9/GI; Agrobacter/GI; MoMo Productions/GI; AJ_Watt/GI; Peter Dazeley/GI; Alex Liew/GI; Science Photo Library/GI; Compassionate Eye Foundation/Gary Burchell/GI; PeopleImages/GI; SolStock/GI; PixeloneStocker/GI; Sigrid Gombert/GI; **Unit 4** XiXinXing/GI; Mixetto/GI; Adastra/GI; Peter Zelei Images/GI; Sunwoo Jung/GI; Yaorusheng/GI; LightFieldStudios/GI; D-Keine/GI; Jamie Grill/GI; FangXiaNuo/GI; **Unit 5** Nikolay Denisov/GI; Chase Dekker Wild-Life Images/GI; K. D. Kirchmeier/GI; Paulo Etxeberria Ramírez/GI; Alavinphoto/GI; Francesco Riccardo Iacomino/GI; Sally Anscombe/GI; Mayur Kakade/GI; Ascent Xmedia/GI; Matteo Colombo/GI; Todd Ryburn Photography/GI; **Unit 6** Westend61/GI; SDI Productions/GI(x2); Teera Konakan/GI; Onurdongel/GI; Maskot/GI; Witthaya Prasongsin/GI; **Unit 7** Fstop123/GI; Carol Yepes/GI; Christian Kober/Robertharding/GI; Yasser Chalid/GI; Tom Werner/GI; Ibnjaafar/GI; Burak Sür/GI; CalypsoArt/GI; **Unit 8** Andrew Bret Wallis/GI; Nazar Abbas Photography/GI; Kelly Cheng Travel Photography/GI; Xavierarnau/GI; Natalia Lebedinskaia/GI; Flashpop/GI; Pixelfit/GI; schlol/GI; **Unit 9** Bortonia/GI; Fotografía de eLuVe/GI; Rockaa/GI; Tetra Images/GI; Carol Yepes/GI; ArtistGNDphotography/GI; miodrag ignjatovic/GI; Edwin Remsberg/GI; NickyLloyd/GI; **Unit 10** Damircudic/GI; Xavier Lorenzo/GI; Morsa Images/GI; Jutta Klee/GI; Kanok Sulaiman/GI; Izusek/GI; Nitat Termmee/GI; Sergio Formoso/GI; BlackCat/GI; David Espejo/GI; Kemter/GI; Mikael Vaisanen/GI; Ariel Skelley/GI

Key GI = Getty Images